40 Music Games to Make and Play

June Tillman

M
MACMILLAN

© June Tillman 1983

All rights reserved. No reproduction, copy or transmission of this publication may be made without written permission.

No paragraph of this publication may be reproduced, copied or transmitted save with written permission or in accordance with the provisions of the Copyright, Designs and Patents Act 1988, or under the terms of any licence permitting limited copying issued by the Copyright Licensing Agency, 33–4 Alfred Place, London WC1E 7DP.

Any person who does any unauthorised act in relation to this publication may be liable to criminal prosecution and civil claims for damages.

First published 1983
Reprinted 1984, 1987, 1989, 1990

Published by
MACMILLAN EDUCATION LTD
Houndmills, Basingstoke, Hampshire RG21 2XS
and London
Companies and representatives
throughout the world

Printed in Hong Kong

ISBN 0-333-32879-5

Acknowledgements

I should like to thank the staff and children of Furzedown Primary School and Ann Wilkins, the headmistress, for trying out the games; Matthew and Nigel for permission to use songs written for their birthdays; Cynthia Raza and Stainer and Bell for permission to use 'Five Little Fieldmice', 'Jungle Calypso' and 'Away to the Stars'; Jack Chatterley for information that led to 'Secret Code'; Wendy Bird for 'What Can It do?'; Diana Thompson and Shirley Winfield for help and advice; Dorothy Taylor for help with the bibliography; my husband and children for their patience and support.

Contents

Introduction
    Why games?   6
    What sort of games?   7
    Materials for the games   8

Rhythm games

Games for the whole class
    The Leader of the Band   11
    The Snake   12
    Secret Messages   13
    The Hike   14
    Boom Boom Clang Clang   15
    Flower Wheel   16
    Sound Strips   18

Games for small groups
    My Mother Said   19
    Twos and Threes   20

Board games
    Rhythm Snakes and Ladders   22
    Rhythm Bingo   24

Music reading games

Games for small groups
    Anyone for Tennis?   28

Board games
    Musical Ludo   30
    Steeplechase   33
    Make a Word   36
    Noisy Children   38
    Crossing the River   40
    Tourne Case   42
    Happy Musical Families   45

Melody games

Games for the whole class
    Down by the River   48
    There's a Brown Girl in the Ring   49
    Four in a Boat   50
    Five Little Fieldmice
    Somebody's Knocking at your Door   51

Games for small groups
    Sound Collage   52

Speed, dynamics and tone colour games

Games for the whole class
    Fast and Slow   57
    The Hidden Bell
    Secret Code   58

Games for small groups
    Change It   59
    What Can It Do?   62
    Opposites   64

Composition games

Games for the whole class
    Conversations   68
    Acky Acky Alphabet   69
    Geographical Music   70
    Musical Telegrams   72
    Sally Beetle   73
    Chordal Adventure   76

Board games
    Jungle Trek   78
    The River   80
    Prehistoric Ramble   82

Glossary   87
List of instruments   91
Bibliography   96

Introduction

Music is concerned with sound — patterns, textures, colours. Certain basic concepts therefore, underlie all music at whatever level— loud/soft, fast/slow, long/short, high/low, having no beat/having a steady beat. Too often in the past music education has been about the written symbols for these sounds and has lost sight of the sound itself. This has resulted in dreary theory lessons spent shunting black dots around five lines in accordance with certain pre-ordained rules that have long since lost touch with the nature of the sound from which they were supposed to be drawn. Many people soon decided that music was not for them, that they were not 'musical', despite the fact that many of them actually enjoyed listening to music — they just couldn't cope with the notation. Had sound been more central to the music curriculum more people might have found in it some relevance; they might have regarded themselves as able to contribute something musical in the same way as they could do in the other arts such as writing and painting.

Certain spheres are the core of music education — *composition, listening* and *performance.* Composition means the arranging or ordering of sounds, listening involves the ability to respond to a piece of music with feeling, while performance is the re-creation (whether on an instrument or singing) of another person's musical intention. There are two allied areas which can contribute to these three spheres: they are often described as specific *skills* (e.g. instrumental technique and the ability to comprehend notation), and *literacy,* which is concerned with information about music — the history of musical style and so on. A good music curriculum includes aspects of the main spheres and introduces the other two areas as required. For example, a group may get to a stage in composition where its members need to write down their pieces, or they may be dissatisfied with their performance because of inadequate instrumental technique. But skills and literacy must always be interlinked with the three main spheres in this way and not become ends in themselves, as they did in the theory classes described earlier. It is on these principles that the games in this book are based.

Games to aid music education fall mainly into two types — games about music and musical games. The first sort are designed to convey information about music (they are concerned with literacy) — composers, families of the orchestra, meanings of terms and signs and so on (*Allegro* [see bibliography] is an example of this type). The games in this book are all of the second type — musical games. They are designed to explore concepts about sound, and if there is a written symbol involved there is always a link with the sound. Sound is the essence of music — the written symbol is merely an aid to it. There is little point in knowing that the first line of the treble clef is E unless you can sing or play it. The games involve listening (an activity central to all musical work), performing, composing, and pure listening (listening for its own sake). It is not possible to lay too much stress on the listening aspect of the games; the teacher should always have an ear to the overall effect of the piece that is being created (especially in such games as 'Jungle Trek', 'Sound Collage', 'Flower Wheel' and 'What Can It Do?').

Nevertheless, in no way do I see this book as any sort of course. The games are intended as supplementary material to the music curriculum. 'Fast and Slow' can be played when that concept is being explored, 'The Snake' when looking at ostinati, 'What Can It Do?' when looking at tone colour and so on. Some can provide the musical work for an integrated studies project.

While none of the games require advanced musical skills, they do demand a varying amount of musical expertise on the part of the teacher. Some require only sensitivity to people and sound (such as 'Conversations', 'Fast and Slow, and 'Acky Acky Alphabet'). Some require the ability to hold a steady beat (such as 'My Mother Said', 'The Snake', 'The Leader of the Band'). In some the beat has to be conducted in some way (such as 'Flower Wheel', 'Chordal Adventure', 'Sound Collage' and 'Boom, Boom, Clang, Clang'). In some a song has to be taught and some singing by the teacher is required (such as in the singing games, 'The Leader of the Band', 'The Snake', 'Twos and Threes' and the composition games). In 'Sound Strips' the teacher can play but may use a record instead.

Sensitivity is the key to these games; I hope that you enjoy them.

Why games?

The basic reason for any game must be because it is fun. The games in this collection will make some of the more repetitive tasks involved in learning music more exciting. The drudgery of naming the notes on the stave, repeating rhythm patterns and so on is taken away when they are carried out in the context of a game like 'Snakes and Ladders'.

Some of the games involve children composing music, exploring sound. Such exploration, whether with the voice or with instruments, is vital to the development of musical concepts but it is difficult to organise. Sometimes there are not enough instruments to go round and the teacher has the task of allocating them in a way that the children accept as fair. There is also the problem of who plays first and the amount of noise involved if everyone explores simultaneously. The composition games (like 'Jungle Trek') and the ones in which the instruments are passed round the circle (like 'Conversations') solve these problems, though the teacher should ensure that everyone has a turn (this is built in to some of the games).

There are games in this book which involve the creation of pieces using chance operations — spinning a spinner, throwing a dice or players choosing what to play from a selection of tunes or rhythms. This technique is in line with developments in contemporary music, with composers using such devices in their compositions, and it prepares children for listening to and participating in these pieces. The game involving choice, 'Sound Collage', demands that the children make sensitive artistic decisions — listening carefully and playing sensitively.

What sort of games?

The games are divided into five categories (though many games involve more than one concept and therefore bridge two or more categories):
1 Rhythm games, in which the games involve the recognition and performance of a variety of rhythms.
2 Music reading games, in which the games aid the further development of music reading skills — the ability to interpret written notes with pitch as well as rhythm.
3 Melody games, in which the emphasis is on performance. This category includes several singing games; these are the oldest type of musical game and are very important in the life of the class — the circle formation creates a feeling of group unity and within it some very old rituals, like choosing a partner, are enacted.
4 Speed, dynamics and tone colour games, in which the games explore these aspects of musical sounds.
5 Composition games, in which the games involve children making up pieces sometimes in response to each other (e.g. 'Conversations', a game which I regard as basic to any work involving children composing because of the sensitivity involved in it), sometimes in accordance with a given structure (e.g. 'Musical Telegrams') and sometimes around a theme (e.g. 'The River').

Within each category the games can be subdivided into games for the whole class, games for small groups and board games. It is hoped that these subdivisions will be useful, although obviously they overlap: many of the games for the whole class can be played by smaller groups, the games for small groups can be played by the whole class in small groups, and many of the board games are games for small groups. Three of the board games are self-checking — 'Noisy Children', 'Crossing the River', and 'Tourne Case' — and can therefore be played by the children with minimal supervision by the teacher; it would be possible to organise a lesson in which some children played these games while the teacher played other games with the rest of the class.

I hope the games in this book will be used as starting points for teachers to make up their own games, for example by adapting the basic principles of a game to a project the class is undertaking. The instructions for each game give the number of players and a guide to the age range of the players, but many of the games can be adapted to suit the stage that the children have reached, starting with a limited number of notes and time values and moving on to a greater number and complexity. Many of the games were originally intended for elementary recorder players.

Materials for the games

All the games demand very simple equipment which is listed at the start of each game. A description of all the instruments mentioned in the book is included on page 87. The boards, wheels and cards should be made out of cardboard of the appropriate size and covered with laminated material. Pupils can contribute to the boards by doing drawings, although some of the more complicated board games are provided in a form and size which can be reproduced easily by tracing.

Many of the games require instruments to be available, although some use voice only; ('Acky Acky Alphabet' and the singing games, for example). Some use only one instrument which is passed round (like 'Fast and Slow') and some need instruments for everyone (although some of these can be very simple like home made shakers, paper rustles, or two stones struck together). Some require skill on a pitched instrument (e.g. violin, recorder), others need only the ability to handle a drum.

Adapt the games in this book to suit your needs; use them as starting points for your own games, your own exploration. Have a good time.

Rhythm games

The Leader of the Band

Objective

To introduce the idea of maintaining a steady beat using body rhythm.

Number of players 4-30

Age 5-9

Materials

None.

To play

The players make a circle. One pupil is chosen as band leader. All the players sing the first verse of this song:

[Musical notation]

1. Oh here stands the lead-er of the whole class band, the whole class band, the whole class band, Oh here stands the leader of the whole class band Fol-low what he/she does.
2. Oh go out and choose a-noth-er lead-er now, lead-er now, lead-er now, Oh go out and choose a-noth-er lead-er now Shake hands with him/her now.

During this the leader does some action in time to the beat of the song, e.g. clap, stamp, finger snap, slap knee. The class copies him.

The players sing the second verse of the song, while the leader shakes hands with one of the circle who takes his place as leader of the band. The class continues to keep the beat and the old leader takes his place in the circle. The class sings the first verse again. The leader finds a new way of keeping the beat which the class copies.

At first let players do anything they like to the beat. When they are used to the game make it a rule that each person must find a new way of keeping the beat. Later the children can use a combination of techniques, e.g.

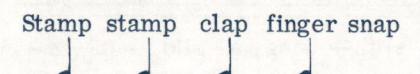

Stamp stamp clap finger snap

Variation

This game can be extended to setting up a rhythmic ostinato pattern, e.g. ♩ ♩ ♩ or ♩ ♩. ♩

At first it will be easiest to clap this but later you could use body sounds for this as well.

The Snake

Objective

To get the children to keep a steady beat with their feet and at the same time to hold a rhythmic ostinato against it.

Number of players 5—30

Age 6—9

Materials

A drum. A large room.

To play

Before you start the game make sure that each player can clap the rhythm of his first name in relation to a steady beat,. e.g.

Say: Melanie

Clap: ♫ ♩

Beat: ♩ ♩

Space the players all over the hall. They sing this song:

The snake comes a-slith-er-ing, a-slid-ing, a-glid-ing,
Made up of rhythms as he goes A-slith-er-ing, a-slid-ing, a-glith-er-ing, a-glid-ing, Who will he choose next?

During the song the teacher walks round the hall in and out of the players keeping a steady beat with his feet and banging a drum like this:

Feet: ♩ ♩ ♩ ♩

Drum: ♩ ♩

At the end of the song the teacher touches a player who joins on behind him walking in time with him and clapping the rhythm of his (the player's) name. At the end of each repetition of the song a further player is added to the snake which eventually includes the whole class.

Secret Messages

Objectives

To imitate a simple rhythm.
To pass a rhythm message correctly from the front to the back of the team.

Number of players 8—30

Age 6—10

Materials

None

To play

Arrange the class in teams, with seven or eight children in each team. Explain that the message to be passed will be:

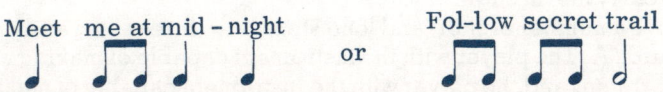

Meet me at mid-night   or   Fol-low secret trail

He claps these two messages, making sure that all the players can clap both.

The teacher taps one of the rhythms on the shoulder of the first child in each team. Each first child taps his rhythm on the shoulder of the child behind him who in turn passes it on, and so on until the last person in each team has the rhythm. He passes it back to the teacher.

The teams that pass the rhythm message correctly win a point. Stress that it is not a race: the important thing is to do it accurately. Repeat the games using the same teams but giving each team a new message.

Other messages you might use are:

En-e-my close at hand

En-e-my planes over-head

Ad-vance in sin-gle file

Wear a dark mac

The Hike

Objectives

To distinguish between long and short sounds.

To introduce crotchets, quavers and minims (in the variations).

Age 6—10

Number of players 5—30

Materials

An instrument capable of playing a long sound, e.g. a cymbal. An instrument capable of producing a short sound, e.g. a woodblock.

To play

One player A stands at the front of the class with his back to everyone else. Two players B and C stand some distance behind and to the side of him:

> A
> B   C

Another player has an instrument capable of making a long sound. A fifth player has an instrument capable of making a short sound.

Everyone recites: I'm going on a hike,
  Will you come too?
  Give me some steps
  To carry me through.

Player A tells B to move a number of short and long steps, e.g. three short and one long. Player B takes these steps towards A. The player with the instrument capable of making a short sound plays while he takes the short steps and the player with the instrument capable of making a long sound plays during the long one.

Everyone then recites the rhyme again. Player A tells player C to move a certain number of short and/or long steps, e.g. two long steps. Player C takes these steps towards A. The players play their instruments with the long and short steps as before.

Everyone recites the rhyme again.

Play continues with instructions given alternately to B and C until one of them reaches player A. He becomes the new player A and the game begins again.

Variations

1 Call the short steps running steps and play them as quavers on the instrument capable of producing a short sound. Call the longer steps walking and link them with crotchets on the instrument capable of producing the longer sound.

2 Later you could introduce jumps and link the longer notes (minims) on an instrument capable of producing a longer sound (e.g. a metallophone).

Boom, Boom, Clang, Clang

Objectives

To hold rhythmic ostinati.

To introduce crotchets, quavers, minims and rests.

Number of players Whole class

Age 6—10

Materials

A large room.

To play

Divide the class into four groups. Each group moves and makes a sound suggested by machine noises, e.g.

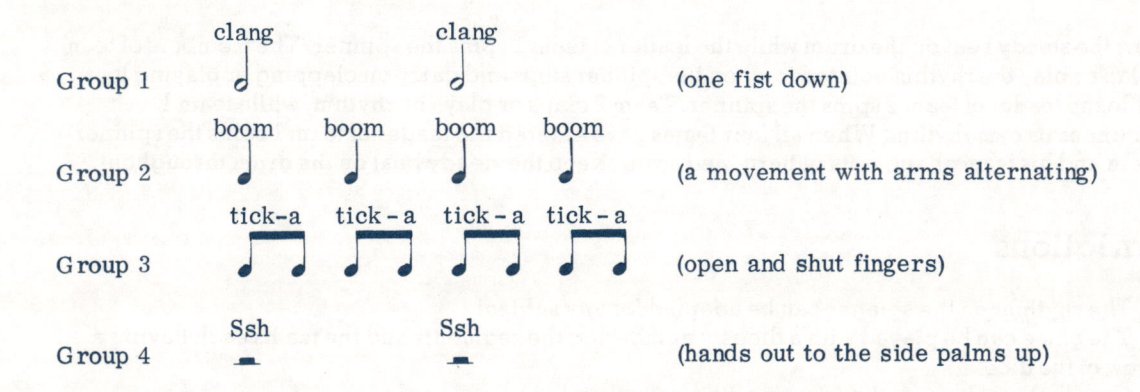

Group 1   clang clang   (one fist down)

Group 2   boom boom boom boom   (a movement with arms alternating)

Group 3   tick-a tick-a tick-a tick-a   (open and shut fingers)

Group 4   Ssh Ssh   (hands out to the side palms up)

The teacher will need to keep a steady beat either visually or aurally to keep the groups together.

Keep changing round until each group has tried each sound.

Variation

Take a strongly rhythmic record (e.g. 'The Grand Old Duke of York', or 'The Typewriter', by Leroy Anderson) and invent ostinati using the movements and the sounds in combinations, e.g.

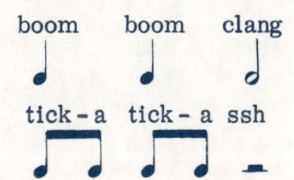

boom boom clang

tick-a tick-a ssh

At first the teacher leads this and the class follow. Then members of the class can take it in turns to lead.

Flower Wheel

Objective

To read and hold simple rhythmic ostinati.

Number of players 4—30

Age 6—11

Materials

A drum for the teacher. Instruments for the children: drums, metal instruments, shakers. Give all the children in each group the same type of instrument. (The game can be played without instruments, by clapping the rhythms). Spinner as illustrated opposite.

To play

Divide the players into four teams, each with a leader. Number the teams one to four. Make sure that all the teams can clap and/or play all the rhythms on the spinner, while you keep a steady beat on the drum.

Start the steady beat on the drum while the leader of team 1 spins the spinner. The members of team 1 clap or play the rhythm pointed to when the spinner stops and carry on clapping or playing it while the leader of team 2 spins the spinner. Team 2 claps or plays its rhythm, while team 1 continues its own rhythm. When all four teams have entered the leader of team 1 spins the spinner again and his team changes its pattern, and so on. Keep the steady beat on the drum throughout.

Variations

1 The rhythms on the spinner can be adapted for any subject.
2 The game can be played with a dice by numbering the segments and the teams each having a throw of the dice.
3 Use rhythms alone on the spinner with no words to help.
4 If the players find rhythms starting before the beat too difficult substitute

♫   ♫   ♫♩   ♪♩♩

'purple sprouting broccoli' for 'nasturtium'.

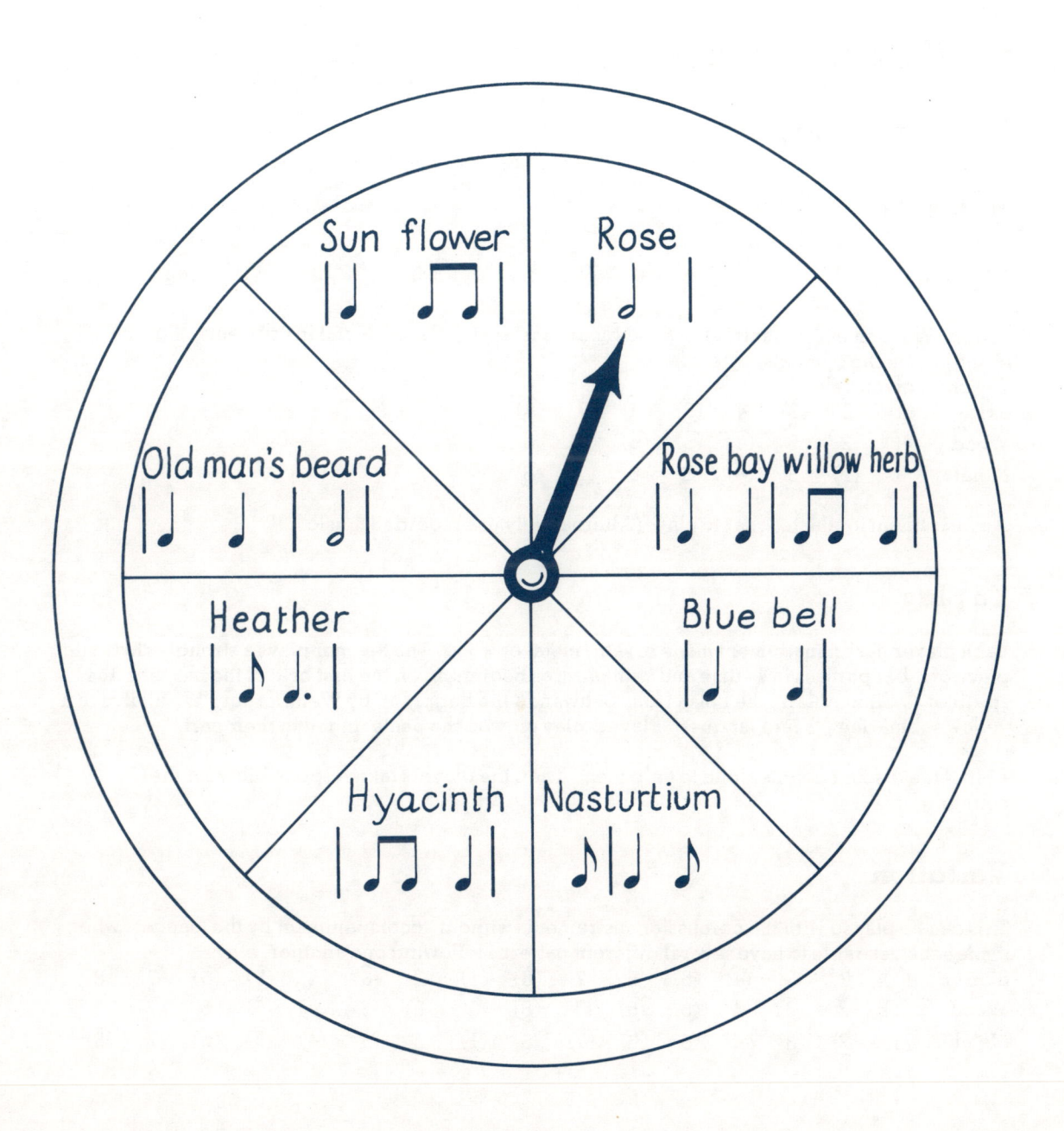

Sound Strips

Objectives

To grasp the basic beat.
To read a simple rhythm.
To read a simple score.
To grasp a eight-beat phrase length.

Numbers of players 3—30

Age 8—13

Materials

Drums. Wooden instruments, e.g. wood block, castanets, claves. Metal instruments, e.g. triangles, Indian cymbals, cymbals.
The chart given below:

Skin	①	2	③	4	⑤	6	⑦	⑧
Wood	①	2	3	④	⑤	⑥	⑦	8
Metal	1	②	3	④	5	6	⑦	⑧

An instrument for the teacher to play. (Alternatively use recorded music.)

To play

Each player has an instrument made of skin, metal or wood. The teacher plays a strongly rhythmic piece of 2-bar phrases in 4–time and with phrases beginning on the first beat of the bar, e.g. the spiritual 'O Sinner Man', the Polka from 'Schwanda the Bagpiper' by Weinberger, 'We all live in a yellow submarine', 'Frère Jacques'. Players play only on the beats ringed in their part.

At first the teacher counts aloud to help them. Then the players take responsibility for the counting.

Variation

This can be played with the percussion instruments without accompaniment by the teacher, when it might be desirable to have several different patterns following one another, e.g.

Skin	①	2	3	④	⑤	6	7	⑧	①	2	③	4	⑤	⑥	⑦	8
Wood	①	2	③	4	⑤	⑥	7	⑧	1	②	3	④	⑤	6	⑦	8
Metal	1	②	③	4	5	⑥	⑦	8	①	2	3	④	⑤	⑥	7	⑧

My Mother Said

Objective

To maintain a steady beat.

Number of players 2 (whole class can do it together in pairs)

Age 5—8

Materials

None

To play

The players recite this rhyme rhythmically:

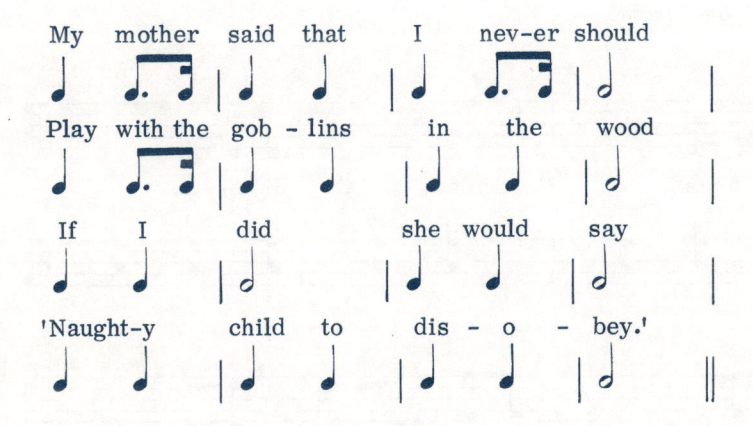

My mother said that I nev-er should
Play with the gob - lins in the wood
If I did she would say
'Naught-y child to dis - o - bey.'

Each player claps his own hands together in time to the beat, then claps together with his partner on the weak beat. Let pairs work out a clapping pattern, alternately clapping their own hands and their partners' hands.

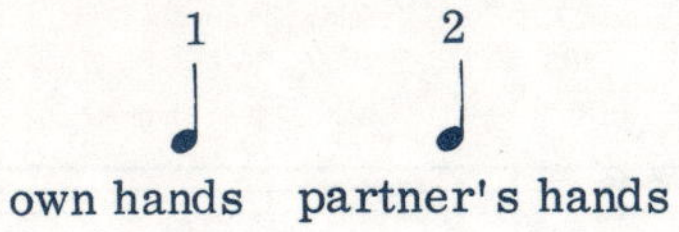

1 2
own hands partner's hands

Variations

1 Any strongly rhythmic rhyme in two time can be used for this.
2 The concept is developed in 'Twos and Threes'.

Twos and Threes

Objectives

To create ostinato patterns involving body rhythms in 2- and 3-time so that pupils experience the difference between these time signatures.
To understand two-part (binary or AB) form.

Number of players 2

Age 7—11

Materials

None.

To play

Teach the players the following song from Africa:

Good day, good day to you, Good day Oh di-pi-du.

Dip, dip dip-i-du di-pi-du, Oh di-pi-du,

Dip, dip, dip, dip di-pi-du di-pi-du, Oh di-pi-du.

Make sure that they can feel the difference between the two sections of the song — the first in 3-time, the second in 2-time. Number the players 1 and 2.

While the teacher sings or plays the song, player 1 invents an ostinato in 3-time involving body rhythms for the first section. Suggest that he uses a stamp on the first beat of each bar (as it is a strong movement) so that the pattern might be

$$\underset{\text{stamp}}{\overset{1}{\downarrow}} \quad \underset{\text{clap}}{\overset{2}{\downarrow}} \quad \underset{\text{clap}}{\overset{3}{\downarrow}}$$

The pattern should be kept simple. Player 2 copies player 1's pattern.

When the second section begins player 1 invents a 2-time pattern, again with a stamp on the first beat of each bar, e.g.

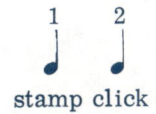

$$\underset{\text{stamp}}{\overset{1}{\downarrow}} \quad \underset{\text{click}}{\overset{2}{\downarrow}}$$

Player 2 copies it.

Change over so that player 2 has a chance to invent the ostinati for player 1 to copy.

Variations

1 The game can be played using two rhythmic tunes — one in 2-time (e.g. 'Baa, baa, black sheep' or 'Polly put the kettle on') and one in 3-time (e.g. 'Lavender's blue' or 'London's burning').
2 More complicated is saying the same rhyme in 2- and 3-time, e.g.

2/4 Good - night, sweet re-pose | Half the bed and all the clothes.

3/4 Good - night sweet repose | Half the bed and all the clothes.

Rhythm Snakes and Ladders

Objective

To teach rhythm reading.

Number of players 2—8

Age 6—13

Materials

A dice. One counter per player.
A board with numbered squares and rhythms written on selected squares; on these squares a snake and a ladder start. The rhythms used will depend on the stage of progress of the pupils but an example of a board used with elementary recorder players is illustrated opposite.

To play

The objective of the game as in ordinary Snakes and Ladders is to reach the final square first. Each player chooses a counter, throws the dice and moves forward the appropriate number of squares. If a player lands on a square with a rhythm on it he must clap that rhythm. If he does so correctly he goes up the ladder, if incorrectly he moves down the snake.

Variation

Tunes of a suitable standard can replace the rhythms on the squares. Players have an instrument and must play the tune to go up the ladder.

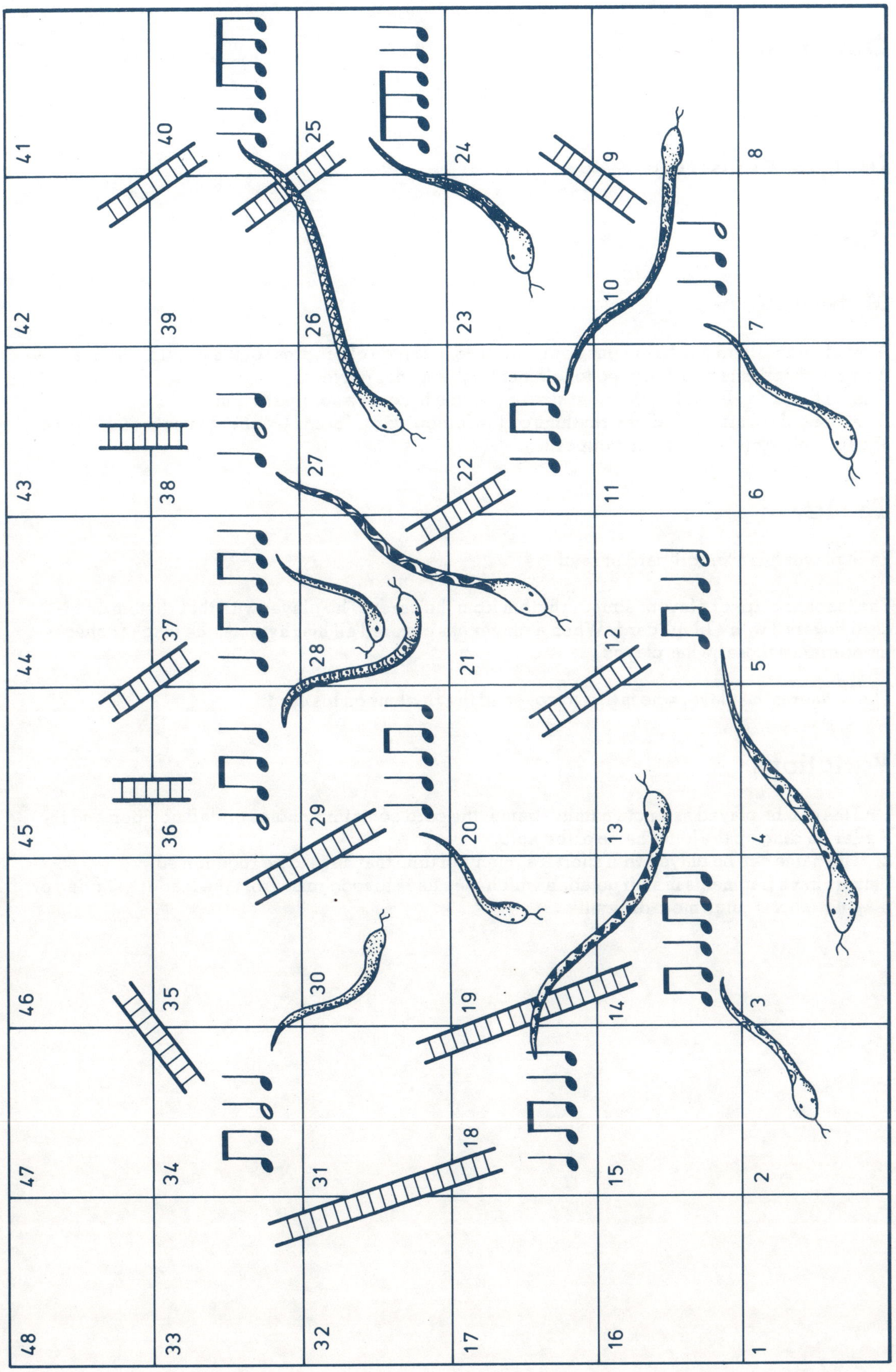
1
2
3
4
5
6
7
8
9
10
11
12
13
14
15
16
17
18
19
20
21
22
23
24
25
26
27
28
29
30
31
32
33
34
35
36
37
38
39
40
41
42
43
44
45
46
47
48

Rhythm Bingo

Objective

To teach rhythm reading.

Number of players 2—15

Age 7—13

Materials

A set of 'bingo' cards with rhythms appropriate to the stage of progress of the pupils. The example illustrated opposite was designed for elementary recorder players.
A set of blank cards each of the right size and shape to cover a single rhythm.
A set of cards containing all the rhythms on the 'bingo' cards for the teacher to use to clap from and as a final check (see illustration opposite).

To play

Each player has a 'bingo' card of rhythms.

The teacher claps or plays or sings a rhythm from the cards. The player with that rhythm on his card covers it with a blank card. When a player has covered all his rhythms, the teacher checks them against those he has played.

The winner is the player who is first to cover all the rhythms on his card.

Variations

1 This can be played as a note naming game, the card containing notes in staff notation and the leader holding up the letter name of the note.
2 The game can be played with short fragments of tune that have to be recognised.
Players have fragments in staff notation which they have to recognise from the leader's singing or playing. This is much more difficult.

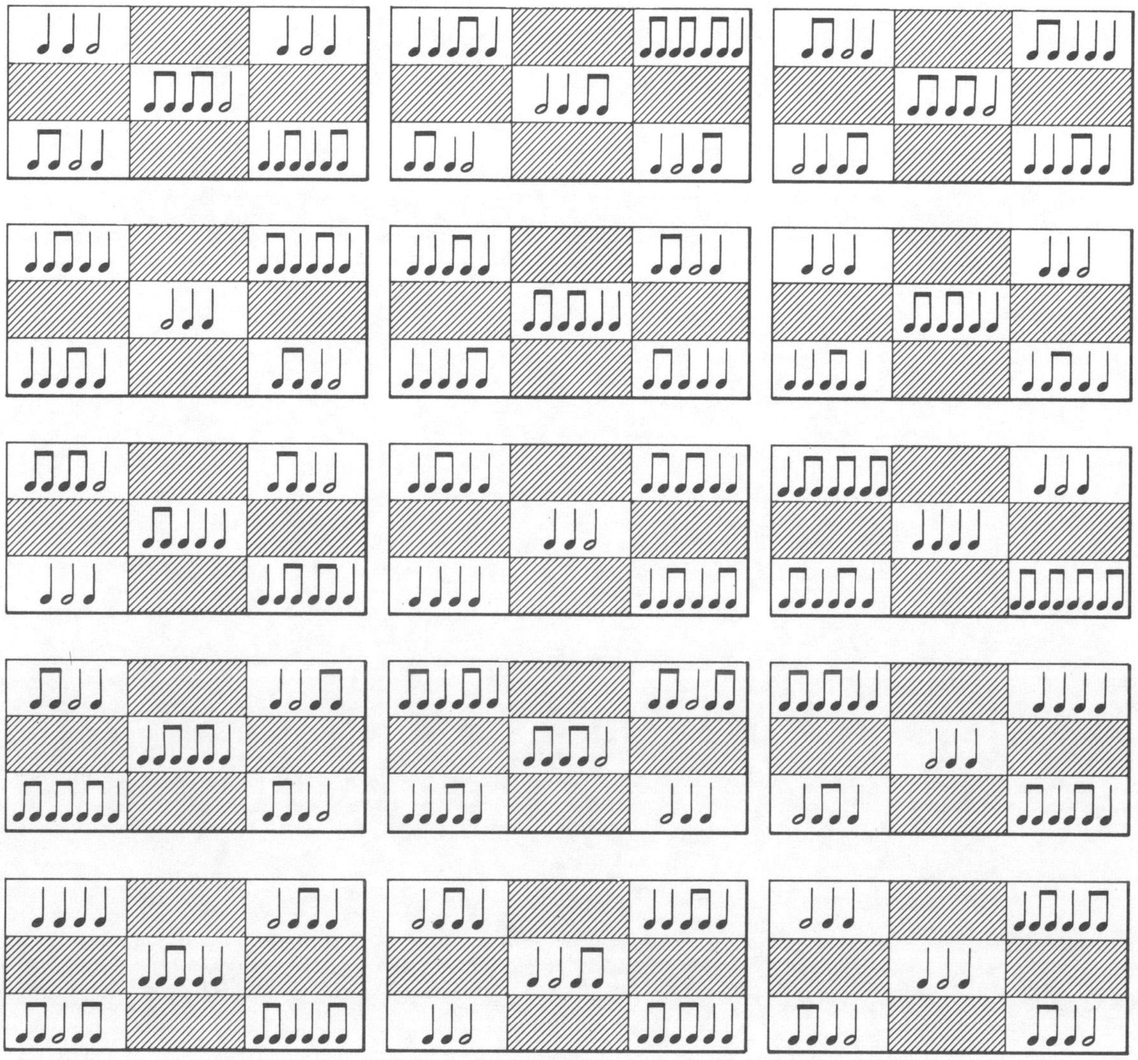

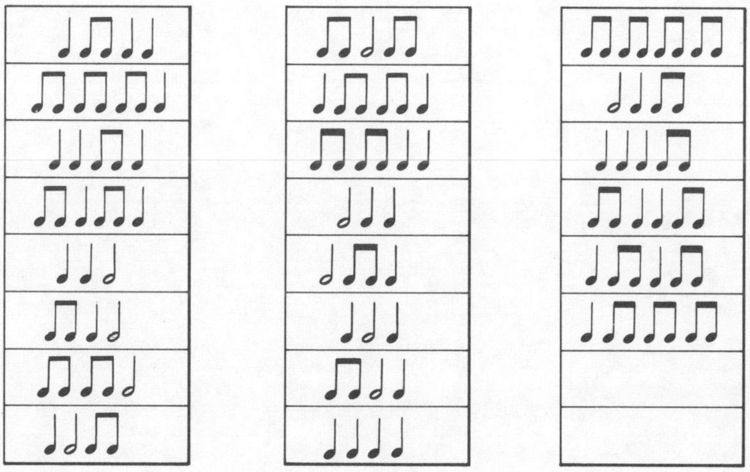

Music reading games

Anyone for Tennis?

Objectives

To enable a player to know a tune really well and be able to start at any place in its course.
To develop sensitivity to the other members of the group.

Number of players 4—12

Age 8—14

Materials

A pitched instrument for each player. Music for each player of a tune that all can play on their instruments.

To play

The players are placed as below and numbered:

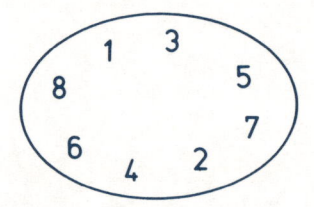

Player 1 plays a section of the tune leaving off where he wishes.
Player 2 has to pick up the tune without a break and he stops where he chooses. Players 3 has to pick up from him, and so on.

If a player fails to pick up accurately he is out of the game and play is adjusted as follows (assuming player two has been knocked out);

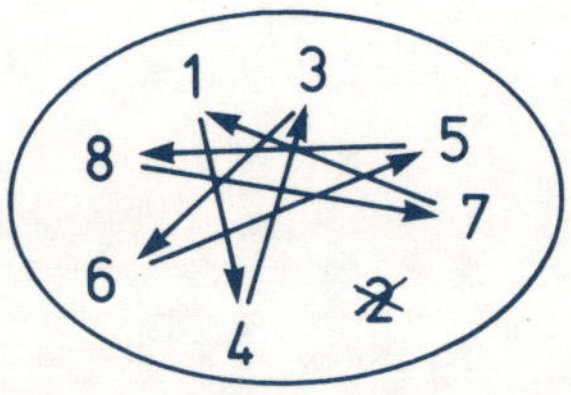

If player 8 is next to go the pattern is as follows:

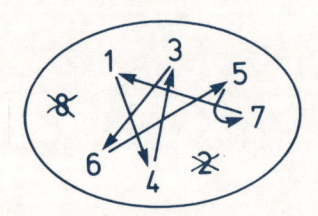

The winner will be the player who can pick up the rhythm from the previous player accurately each time and so remain the last player left in the game.

Variations

1 If you find the order of players too complicated you can go round the circle like this:

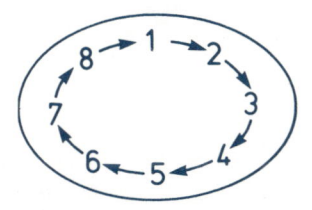

When player 2 is knocked out:

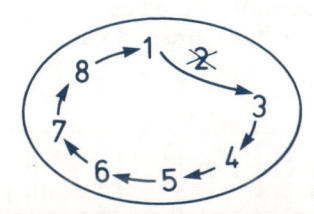

The original order was based on a table tennis game with several players and children find it fun to work out.

2 This game is based on a much more complex one invented by Anthony Milledge for advanced students and incorporating elements of serial technique. It can be played with a simple series using the same pattern as above. Each player has, instead of a tune that he knows a series of notes written in semibreves, e.g. this series for elementary recorder players:

He may play this series in any rhythm he wishes. Again, the next player has to pick up at the point in the series where the previous player finished but he must try and choose a rhythm that will follow well that of the preceding player. The teacher needs to judge how well this has been done. This demands far more skill than the first version of this and demands musical players from age 10 upwards.

With older or advanced players you could attempt a twelve note series using all the notes of the chromatic scale, e.g.

Musical Ludo

Objective

To teach music reading.

Number of players 2-4

Age 7—13

Materials

A set of four counters of the same colour for each player. A dice. A board as in ordinary Ludo but including different coloured squares at various points as illustrated opposite.
Cards in three different colours corresponding with the colours at various points on the Ludo board. Orange cards have rhythms on them, e.g. this set of 12 for pupils who have grasped simple rhythm in 2, 3 and 4–time.

Grey cards have a melody on them corresponding with the stage of development of the players, e.g. this set for elementary recorder players:

	Orange
	Grey
	Green

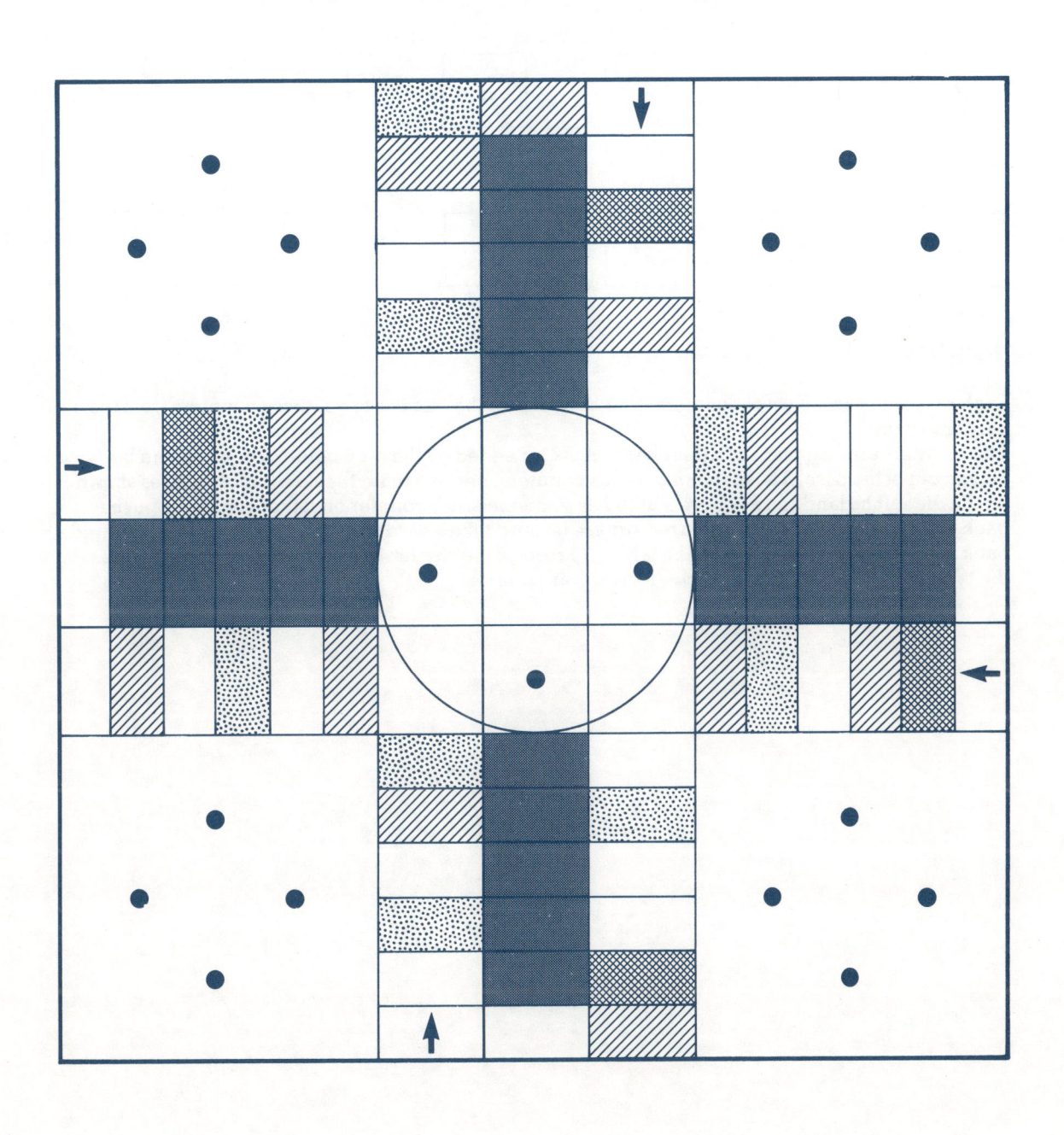

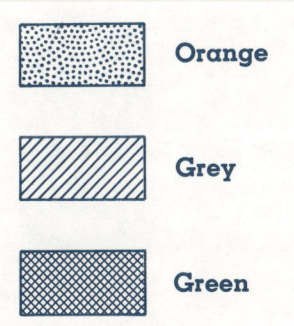

31

Green cards have a term or a sign on them, e.g. this set of 12 elementary signs:

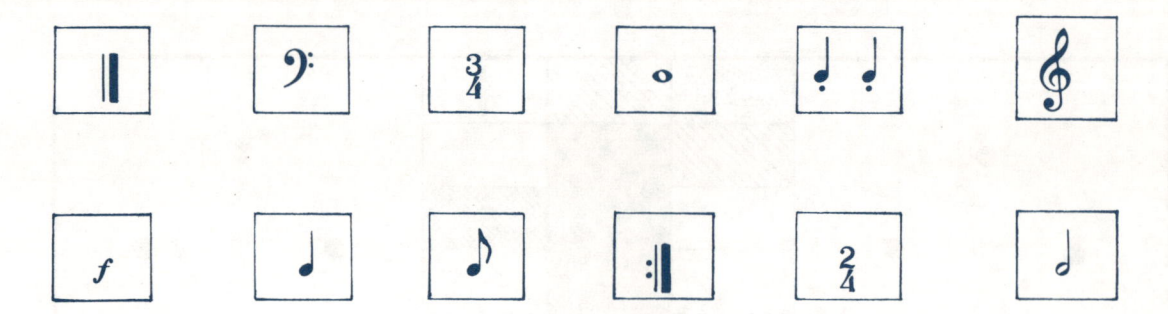

To play

Each player chooses a set of counters. The objective of the game is to get these counters from their base into home.

The counters are first placed in their base. A six is needed on the dice before a counter can be moved out of the base. The player moves his counters, one at a time, the number of squares shown on the dice. If he lands on a square which has someone else's counter on it that counter is pushed back to base. If he lands on a coloured square he must take a card from the appropriately coloured pack which is lying face down on the table. If he claps the rhythm, plays the melody or identifies the term or sign accurately he moves forward six squares.

Steeplechase

Objective

To teach music reading.

Number of players 2—8

Age 7—13

Materials

One horse-shaped counter for each player. An instrument for each player to play. A board as illustrated; obstacles are drawn on the track every four squares.

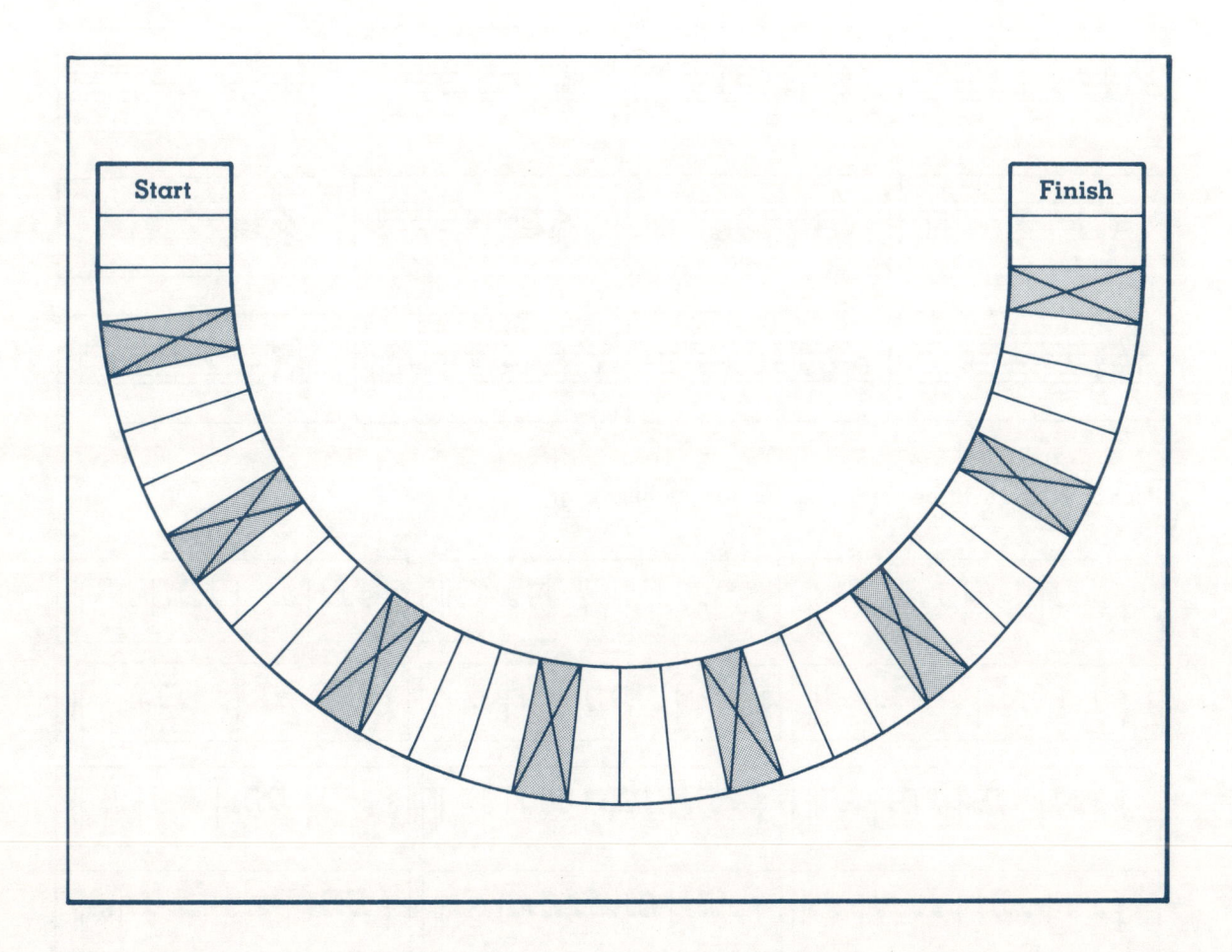

Five packs of cards:
Pack 1, valued at one point, shows two-bar rhythms, e.g.

Pack 2, valued at two points, shows simple melodies of limited range with simple rhythms, e.g.

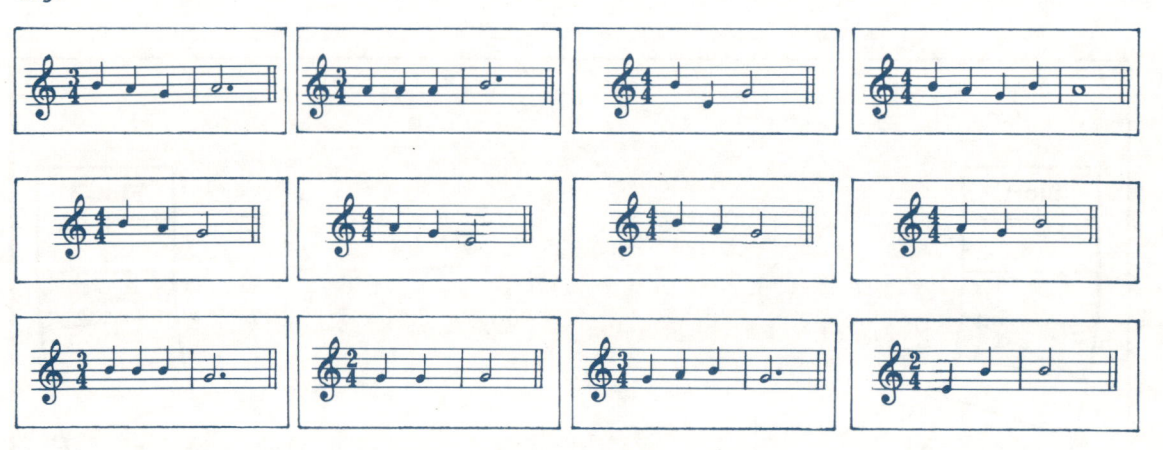

Pack 3, valued at three points, has longer rhythms, e.g.

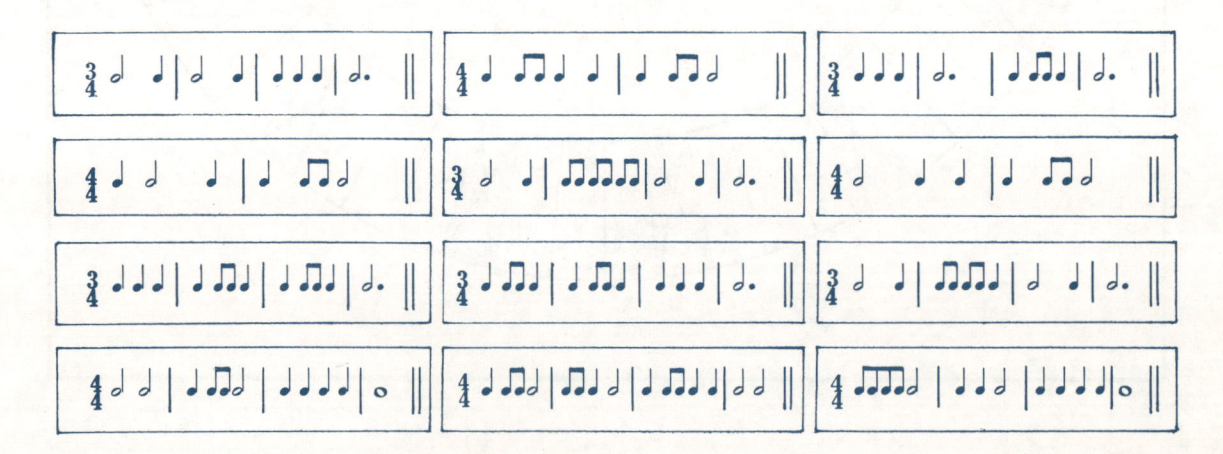

34

Pack 4, valued at four points, shows two-bar melodies using more notes than pack 2, e.g.

Pack 5, valued at five points, has four-bar melodies with at least six notes, e.g.

To play

Each player chooses a different coloured horse-shaped counter. The five packs of cards are laid face down on the table.

The first player decides how many squares he wants to move and takes a card from the pile corresponding to this value. If he claps the rhythm or plays the tune successfully he moves forward the value of the card. If he does it incorrectly he moves back the value of the card.

Players must avoid landing on obstacles. If a player lands on an obstacle he misses a turn. The winner is the first player to finish.

Make a Word

Objective

To teach note reading.

Number of players 2—8

Age 7—13

Materials

Cardboard strips each displaying a word composed of the letters ABCDEFG. The words you use will depend on the notes the players can play. The examples opposite were for a group of elementary recorder players who could play all the notes except F.
Squares of a size that will cover the individual letters of the cardboard strip, each displaying a note in staff notation, e.g.

There should be one square for each letter on the cardboard strips. The notes should be in a clef familiar to the players. (If the letter name is written on the reverse side, players can check their accuracy themselves.)
Blank cardboard bonus squares of the same size as the note squares.
An instrument that each player can play.

To play

The objective of the game is to collect as many cardboard strips, covering squares and bonus squares, as possible.

Lay out the cardboard strips so that all are visible. Place the pile of covering squares face down on the table, with the bonus squares beside them. Each player in turn takes a covering square, works out the letter name of the note and places the square face up over the correct letter on any one of the cardboard strips. When a player lays down the letter that completes the covering of one of the words on the cardboard strips he must play the notes without looking at the letter names underneath.

If he does this correctly he takes the strip and the covering squares. If he uses an interesting rhythm as well he takes one of the bonus squares. If he does it incorrectly he takes only the covering square on the cardboard strip.

At the end of the game each player adds up the total number of separate units he has, e.g. if he has one strip, four covering squares and a bonus square he has a total score of six points for six separate units.

| A | G | E |

| B | A | G |

| G | A | G |

| A | C | E |

| D | E | E | D |

| C | A | G | E |

| B | E | A | D |

| B | A | D | E |

| A | G | E | D |

| E | G | G | E | D |

| C | A | G | E | D |

| B | A | G | G | A | G | E |

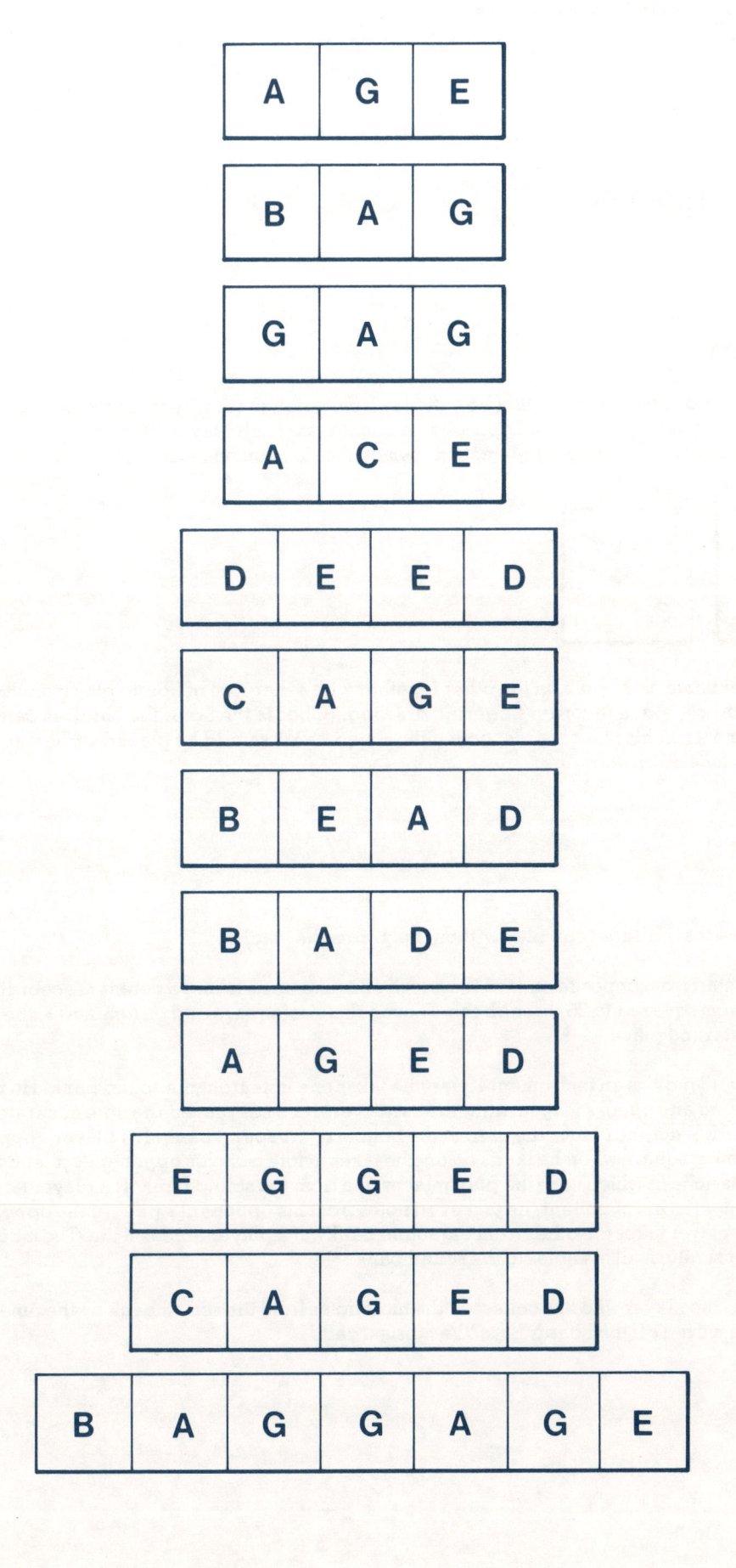

Noisy Children

Objective

To help children name the notes on the stave and play them accurately.

Number of players 2

Age 7-13

Materials

Each player needs an instrument that he can play from notation (e.g. recorder, pitched percussion). A board as illustrated opposite. A counter for each player. A dice.
A bank of 40 cards each with a single note drawn on the stave on one side, e.g.

and the letter name of the note on the other together with a diagram of how to play it on the instrument in use, e.g. a recorder fingering drawing. (Choose the notes the children can play on their instruments.) This pile of cards, called the sound bank, should be placed so that the letter name side is face downwards.

To play

This is a game that children can play without help from the teacher.

The players start from opposite ends of the board and take turns to move counters according to the dice throw from square 1 to 25 through the 'Too much noise' square and on again to 1, the opponent's starting place.

When a player lands on an instrument square he takes one note from the sound bank. He plays the note on the card and checks it by turning the card over. If he has played the note accurately he keeps the card. If not, he places the card at the bottom of the sound bank. If a player's opponent is on an instrument square when he lands on one he takes a note from his opponent's pile, unless the opponent has none in which case the player takes one from the sound bank. If a player lands on the same instrument as his opponent, he takes two notes from his opponent's pile, (if the opponent has only one the player takes the other from the sound bank). If a player lands on the 'Too much noise' square he must return all his notes to the sound bank.

The winner is the player who has collected the most notes from the sound bank by the time both players have moved off the board; he is 'the noisiest child'.

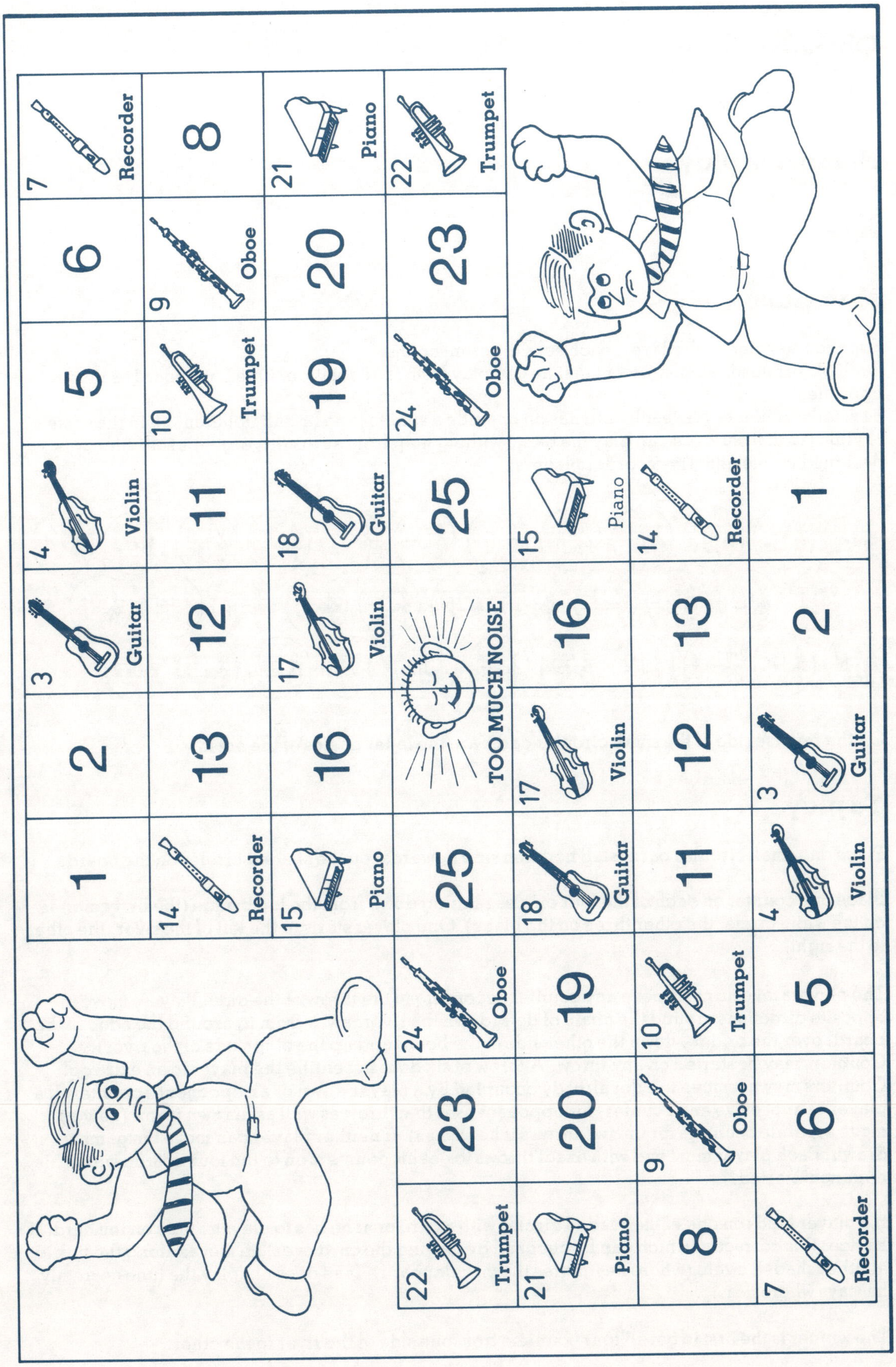

1
2
3 Guitar
4 Violin
5
6
7 Recorder
14 Recorder
13
12
11
10 Trumpet
9 Oboe
8
15 Piano
16
17 Violin
18 Guitar
19
20
21 Piano
25
TOO MUCH NOISE
25
24 Oboe
23
22 Trumpet
22 Trumpet
23
24 Oboe
21 Piano
20
19
18 Guitar
17 Violin
16
15 Piano
8
9 Oboe
10 Trumpet
11
12
13
14 Recorder
7 Recorder
6
5
4 Violin
3 Guitar
2
1

Crossing the River

Objective

To help children to play simple tunes accurately from staff notation.

Number of players 2

Age 7—13

Materials

Four counters for each player, each set a different colour.
Each player needs an instrument that he can play from staff notation. One base board as illustrated opposite.
34 small circular cards: each card has on one side a simple tune in staff notation, all in the same rhythm (so that children can play the game without help from an adult), e.g. this set which was designed for elementary recorder players:

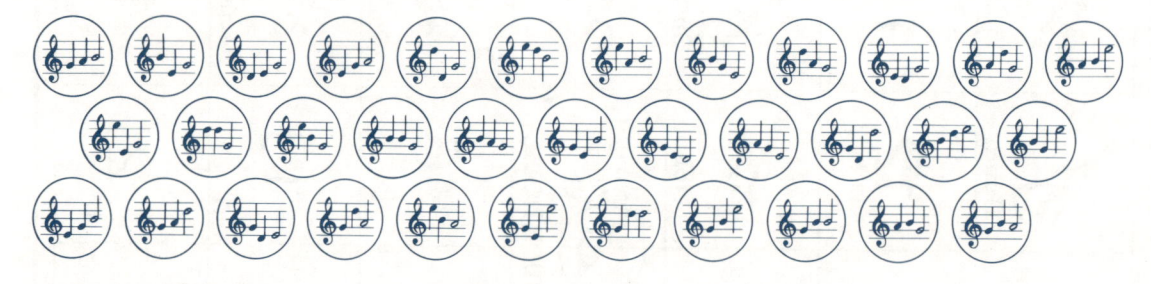

On the reverse side of the small circular cards are the letter names of the notes.

To play

Place one small circular card (staff notation side upwards) on the shaded circles on the board.

Place one counter on each of the four circles ranging down from the top bridge (the first counter on the white circle, the other three on the black). One player starts to the left of the river, the other to the right.

The players take turns to move any counter according to the throw of the dice. Players move in opposite directions around the chain of dots (down the river, away from it, around the edge of the board, over the bridge, down the other side of the board and up the other side of the river). Counters may be started on any throw. A throw of six does not entitle the player to an extra go. Counters may not move to a dot already occupied by a player's own or an opponent's counter. If a player cannot move any counter, his opponent uses that throw as well as his own throw (he may move separate counters for the two throws if he wishes). If neither player can move the game is drawn. Each player must end with exact throws to get his counters on to the four dots on which his opponent started.

If a player lands on one of the shaded circles with a card on it he has to play the tune on the card. If he does this correctly (which can be checked by turning the card over) he moves along the link to another shaded circle (where he ignores the circular card). If he does not play the tune correctly he stays where he is.

The winner is the first to get all four counters from one side of the river to the other.

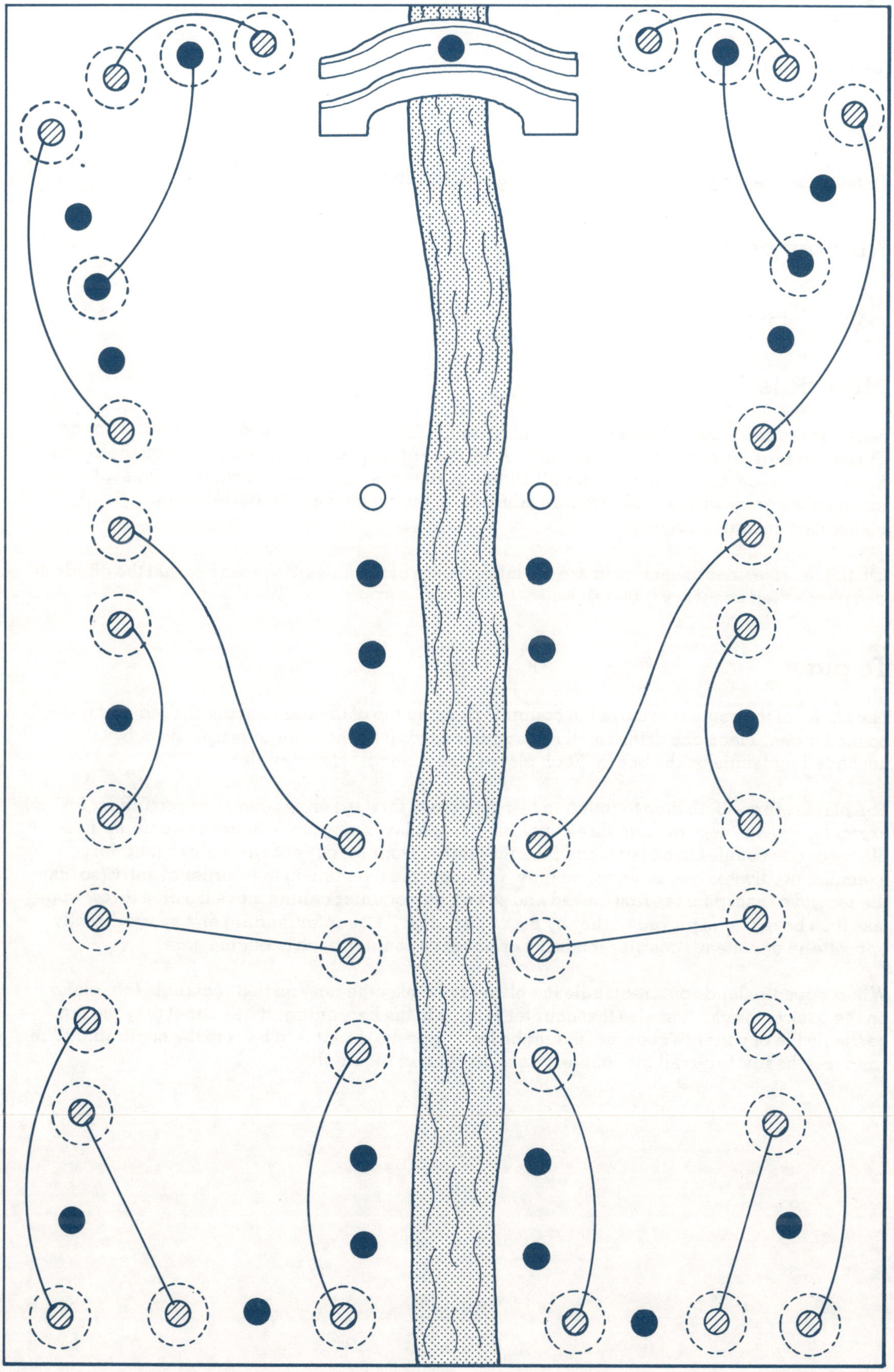

Tourne Case

(based on an old French game)

Objective

To help children to play simple tunes accurately from staff notation.

Number of players 2

Age 7—13

Materials

Each player needs an instrument he can play from staff notation. A board as illustrated opposite. Three counters for each player. Two dice. A set of cards the size of the rectangles on the board. Each card has on it a simple tune in staff notation (all tunes with the same rhythm so that children can play the game without help from an adult), e.g. the set on page 44 designed for elementary recorder players:

On the reverse sides of each card are the letter names of the notes of the tune so that the children can check their accuracy themselves.

To play

The object of the game is to move the counters from the top of the board to the shaded rectangles on the bottom. Place one of the small rectangular cards (staff notation side up) on each unshaded rectangle on the board. Each player takes one row of rectangles.

The players throw both dice together in turn and move forward either one or two counters: for example, on a throw of two and three totalling five, a player may move either one counter five places or one counter two places and the other three. Doubles count as a single so that, for example, two fives is one move of five only. Counters must remain in their order of entry (so that the second cannot pass the first moved and so on); so a counter cannot move if a dice throw would take it on beyond one played earlier by the same player. A counter landing on a space directly opposite an opponent's counter sends the opponent's counter back to begin again.

When a counter lands on a rectangle the player must play the tune on that rectangle (checking it on the back of the card) or else that counter returns to the beginning. If he cannot play the tune correctly the opponent's counter (should he land opposite) is not sent back to the beginning. The winner is the first to get all his counters on to his shaded rectangle.

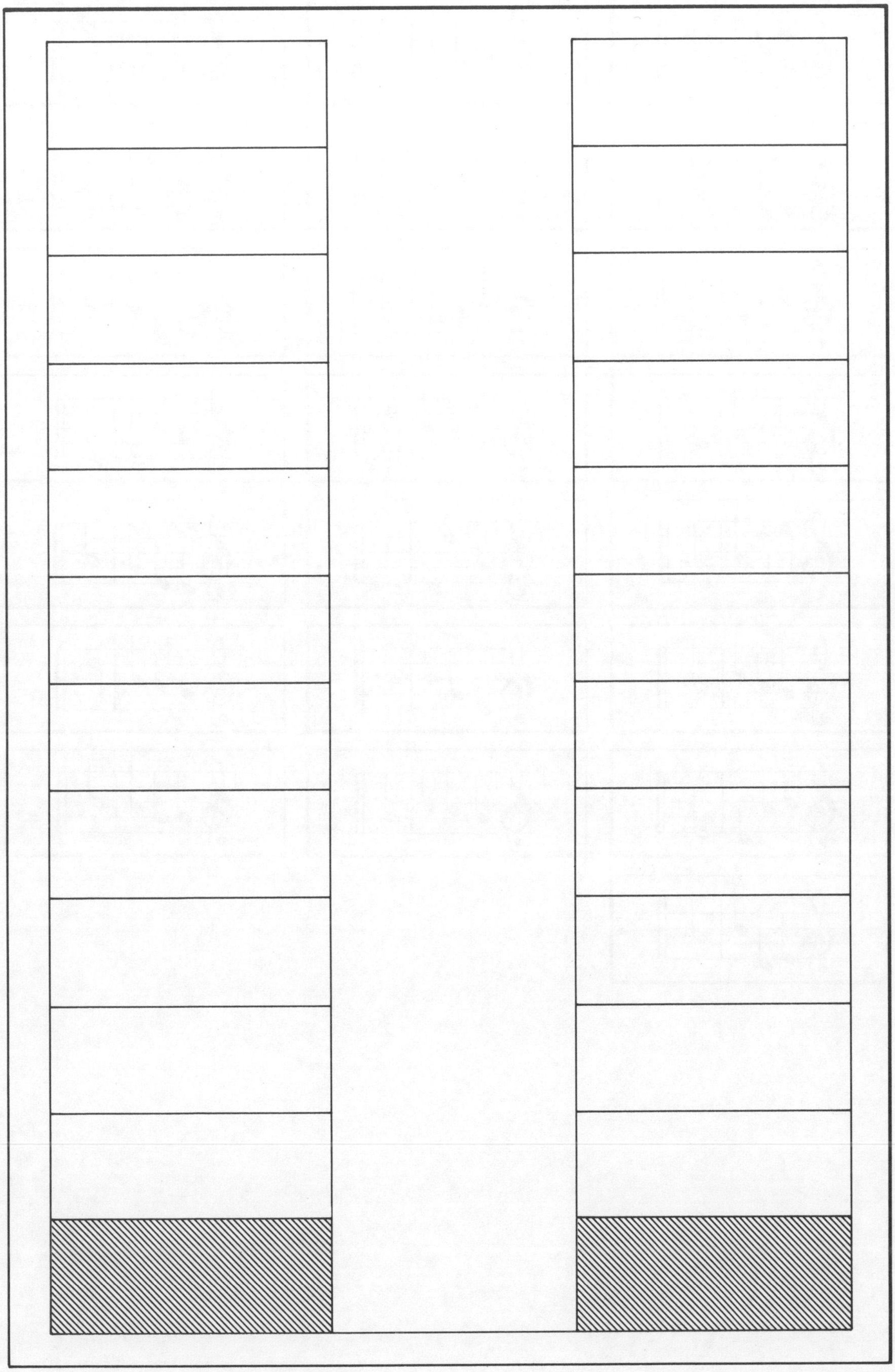

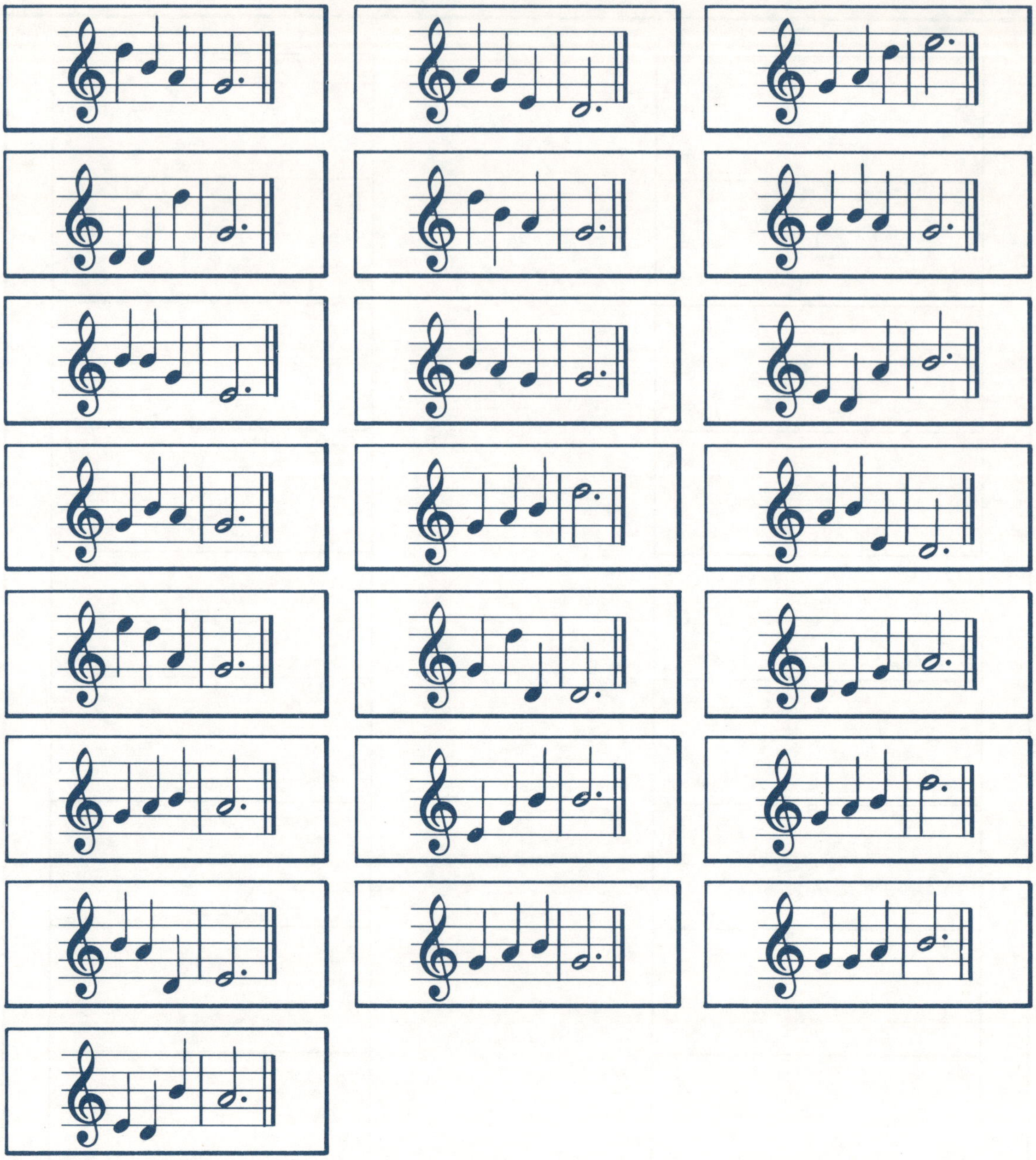

Happy Musical Families

Objective

To teach a knowledge of common signs used in music.

Number of players 4 (or more if more tunes are used)

Age 9—13

Materials

Choose four tunes the children know. Write out the opening so that the total number of signs involved in it is 19, e.g.

London's burning

Happy birthday

There's a hole in my bucket

Au claire de la lune

Make:
One complete strip of each tune (but without the title or the lines dividing the signs). A second strip of each tune, the same size as the first but cut it into the 19 sign units, so that each unit looks something like these:

Four blank cards each the same size as a sign unit, which can be used in place of any of the sign unit cards.
Each player needs an instrument on which he can play the tunes.

To play

Deal out the complete strips, one to each player. Deal seven of the sign unit cards to each player and put the rest face down in a pile in the middle.

Each player lays in front of him under the complete tune all the units he has that are in his tune, e.g.

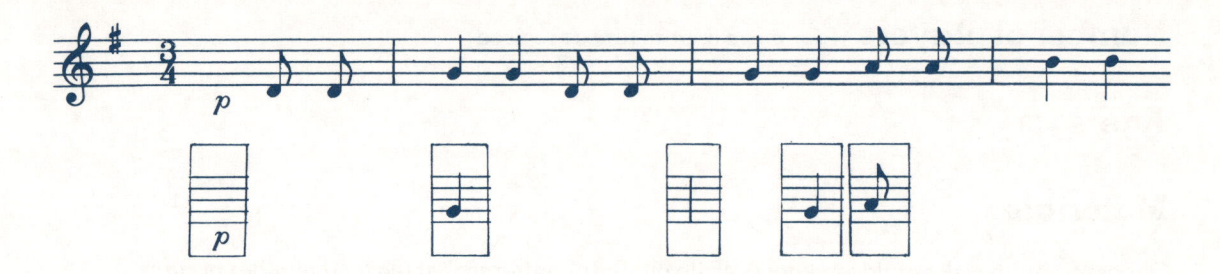

The player who has the most signs for his tune starts.

The first player asks any other player for a sign that he needs, e.g. 'Have you got a crotchet G?' If the other player has it he must give it up. The first player lays down the sign in its place under his tune. His go finishes when the player he has asked has not got the required sign. He then takes from the pile in the middle enough cards to make his hand up to seven.

While the next player has his go the first player may lay down any more signs that he has just drawn from the pack which fit his tune. A blank card may be used for any sign card but once put down it cannot be taken up and changed. Players may not ask for blank cards.

The first player to complete his tune, play it and name it is the winner.

Melody games

Down by the River

(British singing game)

Objective

To encourage the children to sing and move in time to the music.

Number of players 5—30

Age 4—7

To play

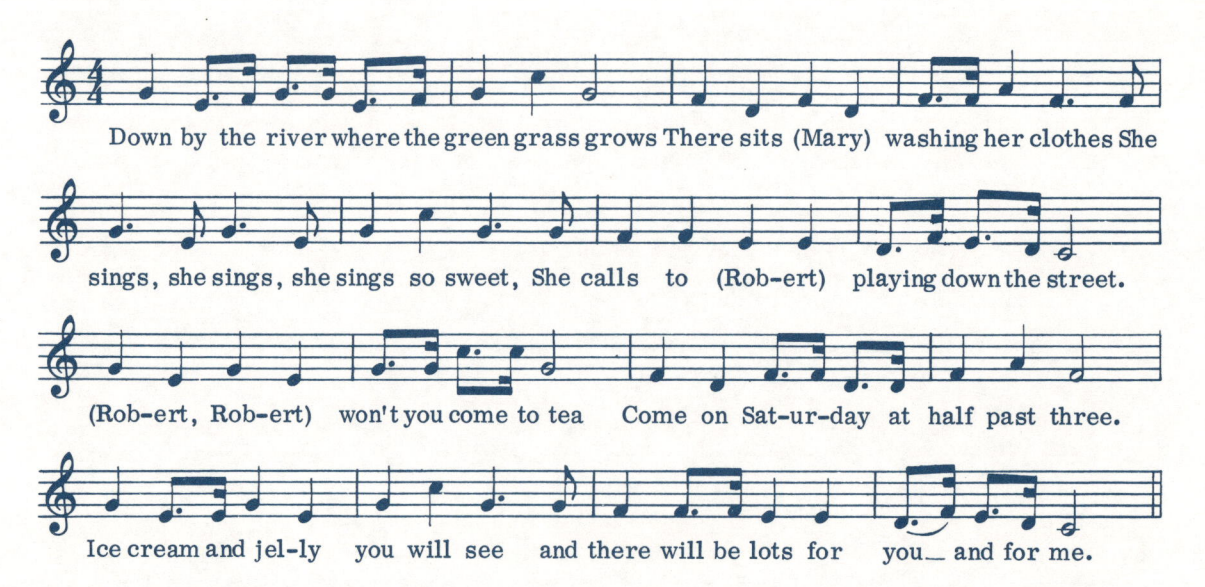

Down by the river where the green grass grows There sits (Mary) washing her clothes She sings, she sings, she sings so sweet, She calls to (Rob-ert) playing down the street. (Rob-ert, Rob-ert) won't you come to tea Come on Sat-ur-day at half past three. Ice cream and jel-ly you will see and there will be lots for you and for me.

The children make a ring with one child in the middle. Ask him to decide who he is going to invite to tea so that you know which name to put in later on in the verse. All walk or skip round the centre child singing the first half of the verse. (This is a very rhythmic game so you can insist that they move in time to the music.) During the second half of the verse the centre child's friend joins him in the middle and they skip or walk round together. The game continues, adding a new friend each time the verse is sung, until the outer circle is too small to contain the inner circle.

There's a Brown Girl in the Ring

(Caribbean singing game)

Objective

To encourage the children to sing and move in time (and in an original way) to the music.

Number of players 5—30

Age 4—7

To play

1. There's a brown girl in the ring, There's a brown girl in the ring, Fa la la la la la Brown girl in the ring, Fa la la la la She likes the sugar and I like plum.
2. Then you show me your motion, Then you show me your motion, Fa la la la la la Show me motion, Fa la la la la She likes the sugar and I like plum.
3. Then you wheel and take your partner, Then you wheel and take your partner, Wheel and take your partner, Fa la la la la She likes the sugar and I like plum.

The children form a circle with one in the middle. During the first verse the centre child skips round inside the circle while the outer circle walks round singing. During the second verse he does a funny walk or action of some kind which the children in the outer circle imitate while they sing. During the third verse the centre child chooses a partner and skips round with him while the children in the outer circle sing and skip round. The partner becomes the next brown girl or boy, and the song is repeated.

Four in a Boat

(North American singing game)

Objective

To encourage the children to sing and move in time to the music.

Numbers of players 10—30

Age 4—7

To play

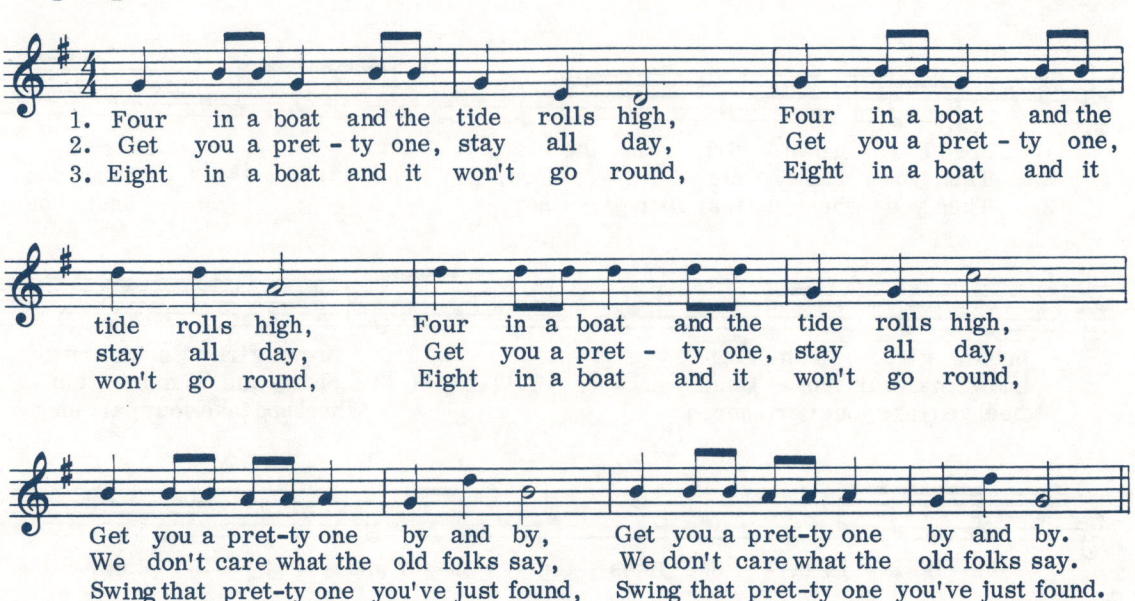

1. Four in a boat and the tide rolls high, Four in a boat and the tide rolls high, Four in a boat and the tide rolls high, Get you a pret-ty one by and by, Get you a pret-ty one by and by.

2. Get you a pret-ty one, stay all day, Get you a pret-ty one, stay all day, Get you a pret-ty one, stay all day, We don't care what the old folks say, We don't care what the old folks say.

3. Eight in a boat and it won't go round, Eight in a boat and it won't go round, Eight in a boat and it won't go round, Swing that pret-ty one you've just found, Swing that pret-ty one you've just found.

The children form a circle. Four girls form a small circle in the centre of the main circle. During the first verse both circles skip round. During the second verse the outer circle stands while the four girls choose four boys as partners. During the third verse the partners skip in pairs while the outer circle skips round again. The four boys form the inner circle for the next round of the game.

Five Little Fieldmice

Objective

To encourage the children to sing, and explore the drama of the song. (It also teaches subtraction)

Number of players 14—30

Age 4—7

To play

*Five little field mice fast asleep
All in a huddle and all in a heap
A tawny owl came by and gave a hoot
and the first little mouse said 'Scoot'.*

The players make a large circle with five children 'asleep' in the middle. One child is chosen to be tawny owl and is outside the circle. The circle walks round singing the first two lines of the song. On the third line the circle stops and drops hands. The tawny owl comes in through one of the holes and touches one of the fieldmice who jumps up and finds a place in the circle, while the children sing the last line of the song. The tawny owl goes outside the circle and the game continues until all the fieldmice have been 'caught'.

Somebody's Knocking at your Door

Objectives

To explore antiphonal effects and encourage children to sing on their own.

Number of players 5—30

Age 6—10

Materials

None.

To play

The players sit in a circle and sing the song below. Everyone sings the parts marked ALL; the first time through the teacher sings the SOLO part, putting the name of one of the players at 'Susan'.

*All: Somebody's knocking at your door, Somebody's knocking at your door.
Solo: Oh ___ (Susan) Why don't you answer?
All: Somebody's knocking at your door.*

The chosen child (Susan) sings the solo part the next time round, naming a different person, who will take over from her when the song is repeated.

51

Sound Collage

Objectives

To build up a texture using different tunes and rhythms.
To give pupils an opportunity to perform a piece involving free choice on the part of the performer. To encourage pupils to be sensitive to what is going on around them and make sensitive artistic decisions.
To create a feeling for four- and eight-bar phrases.

Number of players 4—14

Age 10—14

Materials

Enough duplicated sheets as illustrated for each player to have one. Rhythm instruments (although these parts may be clapped), one for each player. Pitched instruments such as recorders or glockenspiels (although you could use the rhythms alone), one for each player. A conductor.

To play

Make sure each child can play all the lines on the sheet. It is important that each pupil can do this on his own as he has to hold his tune against all the others.

The conductor beats a steady two beats in a bar throughout, indicating groups of four bars, e.g. with an extra down beat with the other hand.

Each player can start *either* by playing the asterisked line on the collage *or* with four or eight bars rest. If he chooses to play he must rest for four or eight bars when he has finished his line. If he chooses to rest, he plays any line of the collage at the end of his rest.

The piece proceeds with each player playing for four or eight bars according to which pattern he has chosen and then resting for four or eight bars as he chooses. He may choose any pattern he likes, this choice being made by listening to what is already going on and choosing what will fit best. For example, if there are all rhythms he might choose to insert a melody or may decide that this section of the piece is best kept all rhythms. If everyone is playing the shorter tunes he may choose to insert one of the longer more prominent tunes. The players must keep within the four-bar or eight-bar phrase structure. A player can repeat any pattern.
The piece can finish either when the conductor decides or when all the players have performed all patterns.

Variations

1   Use clapping, rather than rhythm instruments, for the rhythmic parts.
2   Use clapping only, for both rhythms and tunes.
3   Use rhythm instruments only, using just the rhythm of the pitched parts. To give a greater element of choice each player could have two instruments from which he can choose one at any given time, again listening to what will sound well with what is being played already.
4   Omit the resting periods, each player going straight from one line to the next. In this case, if you are using both pitched and rhythm parts it is best to clap them because of the difficulty of picking up the new instrument in time.
5   If the given sound collage is too difficult you can invent one of your own using the notes of a single chord, e.g. G B D for recorders or E G B for guitars of D F# A for violin.

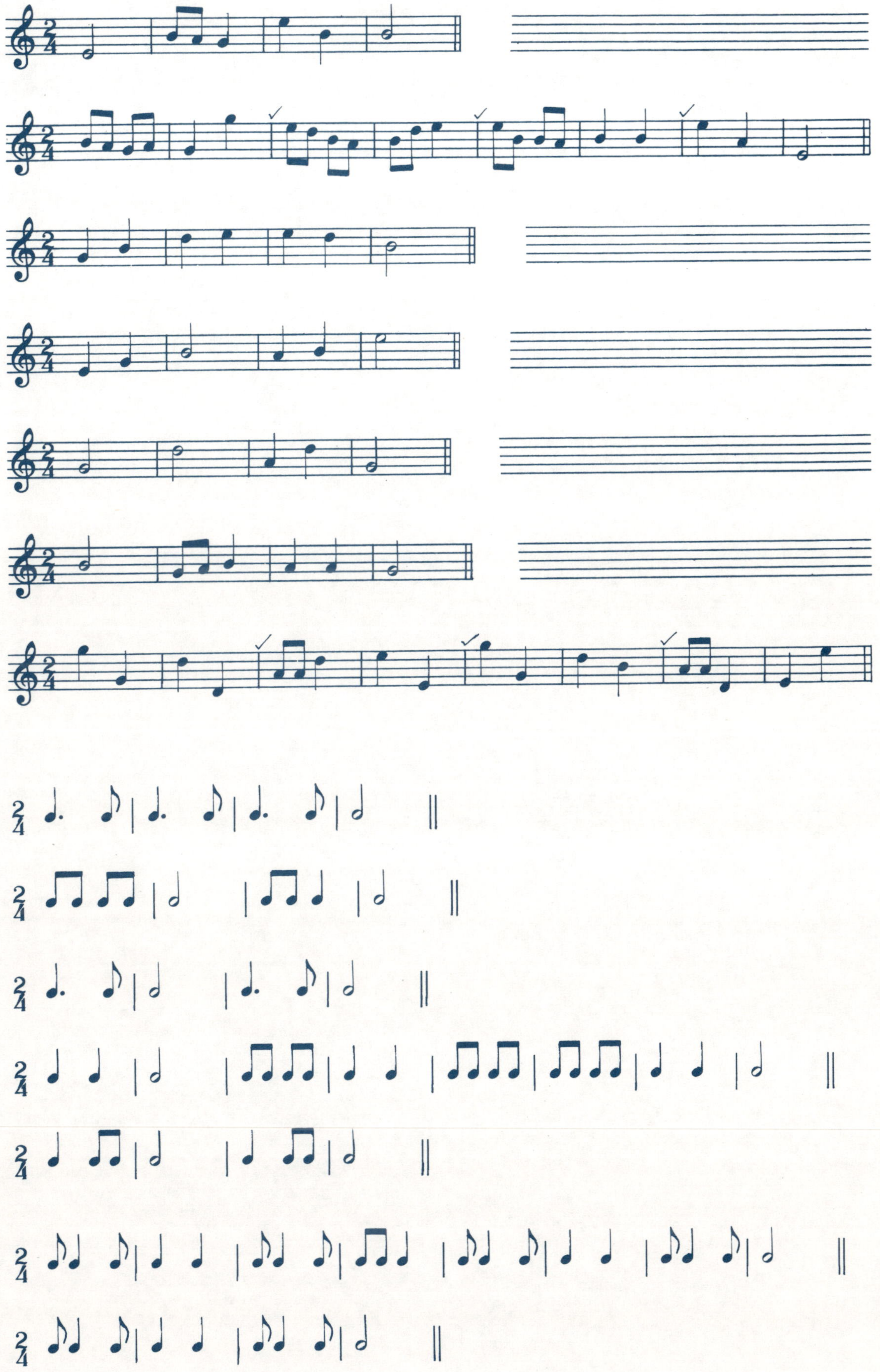

Speed, dynamics and tone colour games

Fast and Slow

Objective

To distinguish between and play fast and slow sounds.

Number of players 4—30

Age 5—9

Materials

Any musical instrument on which you can play fast and slow easily, e.g. a drum or claves, but not a triangle which is difficult to play fast.

To play

Sit the children in a circle. Pass the instrument round while all recite:
Fast and slow,
Fast and slow,
See how it goes.
Whoever has the instrument when the rhyme stops plays fast or slow and the rest of the class claps with him. (Children often need encouragement and help to play slowly.)

Variation

Revise the rhyme so that it runs:
Fast and slow,
Loud and soft,
See how it goes.
Then the player can play fast and loud, fast and soft, slow and loud or slow and soft. The class imitates the player as before but a discussion can follow as to which of these alternatives was chosen.

The Hidden Bell

Objective

To hear and locate very small sounds.

Number of players 6—30

Age 6—8

Materials

A small bell. A large room.

To play

One player leaves the room. The remaining children spread all over the hall with their hands behind their backs. One of them has the bell behind his back. The child outside comes in and the one with the bell makes very small sounds with it. The first child has to guess who has the bell. When the bell ringer has been correctly identified he goes out of the room. The teacher chooses a new bell ringer and the game is repeated.

Secret Code

Objectives

To listen carefully.
To perform accurately in response to a signal from a conductor.

Number of players 8—30

Age 8—13

Materials

A recorder, a cymbal, bells, a stringed instrument, a shaker, a voice and a drum (You can construct your own code using whatever instruments you have available.) Pencil and paper for all the listeners. The code (see below) written up on a board for all to see.

	1	2	3	4
Recorder	A	B	C	D
Cymbal	E	F	G	H
Bells	I	J	K	L
Stringed	M	N	O	P
Shaker	Q	R	S	T
Voice	U	V	W	X
Drum	Y	Z		

To play

The instrument players and a conductor go out of sight of the rest of the children. The conductor decides on the message to be coded. Here are some suggestions: Music is for everyone; All sing together; I have rhythm; Let us sing; Music has charms.

The conductor signals to the appropriate musicians how many notes to play for each letter of the message. For example, the word 'music' is one note on the stringed instrument, one on the voice, three on the shaker, one on the bells and three on the recorder. He should leave gaps between the words and shorter gaps between the letters. The rest of the class decodes the sounds and writes the letter down to form the message. (There needs to be absolute silence as one missed note makes the whole message wrong.)

Change It

These games in small groups involve the creation of a piece which is then changed in some way.

Age 6—10

Machinery Games

Five games in which the children imitate the noise of machinery getting faster, slower or louder.

Machinery game 1

Objective

To maintain a steady pulse.

Number of players 3

Materials

A drum for one player in each three.

To play

One player in each three holds a steady beat on the drum. The other two make rhythmic machinery movement accompanied by a machinery noise.

Machinery game 2

Objective

To get gradually faster.

Number of players 3

Materials

A drum for one player in each three.

To play

As in the first game but this time imagining that the machinery is gradually starting up until it reaches working speed.

Machinery game 3

Objective
To get gradually slower.

Number of players 3

Materials
A drum for one player in each three.

To play
As in the first game but starting at working speed and gradually slowing down.

Machinery game 4

Objective
To get gradually faster and slower.

Number of players 3

Materials
A drum for one player in each three.

To play
Combine the last two games so that the machinery gradually starts up, reaches working speed, works for a while, and then slows down.

Machinery game 5

Objective
To get suddenly louder.

Number of players 3

Materials
A drum for one player in each three.

To play

As in the first game with one player in each three holding a steady beat and two making machinery movement and noise. This time they do it at first as if the factory door is shut. Then they imagine someone opens the door and you hear the machinery at full blast.

Vehicle Game

Objective

To get gradually louder and softer.

Number of players 2

Materials

A simple percussion instrument for one player in each pair.

To play

One in each pair plays a pattern to represent some form of transport. The other moves like the vehicle. Then they imagine that the vehicle is approaching, passing and departing, and modify their pattern accordingly.

The Flower

Objective

To get gradually slower and quieter.

Number of players 2

Materials

One pitched percussion instrument with the pentatonic scale left on, e.g. C D E G A. One unpitched instrument.

To play

One player invents a tune on the pitched instrument to represent the flower. The player of the unpitched instrument invents an ostinato pattern that will go with it; this can be simply playing on the beat. They imagine the flower is dying and make the piece get quieter and slower.

What Can It Do?

Objective

To explore the possibilities of various instruments.

Number of players 2—6

Age 6—11

Materials

One instrument for each of the players. These can range from home made shakers to pitched instruments. A counter for each player. A dice.
One base board as illustrated opposite.

To play

Each player makes a soft continuous sound on his instrument while the other instruments have their turns.

The first player throws the dice and moves to the appropriate square. He uses his instrument to carry out the instruction written on that square. If he thinks that his instrument cannot produce the sound required of it, e.g. a wood block being asked to produce a joined up sound, then he just continues his soft continuous sound through his go, and does not carry out the specific instruction. Each player must wait for his go until the previous player has finished and reverted to the continuous sound. Play gradually stops as the players reach the end of the board.

The teacher and players need to listen carefully to the overall effect of this piece — for example to check that the continuous sound does not obliterate a soft sound required by the board.

Variation

The board can be made more sophisticated by substituting rhythmic notation for the longs and shorts so that:

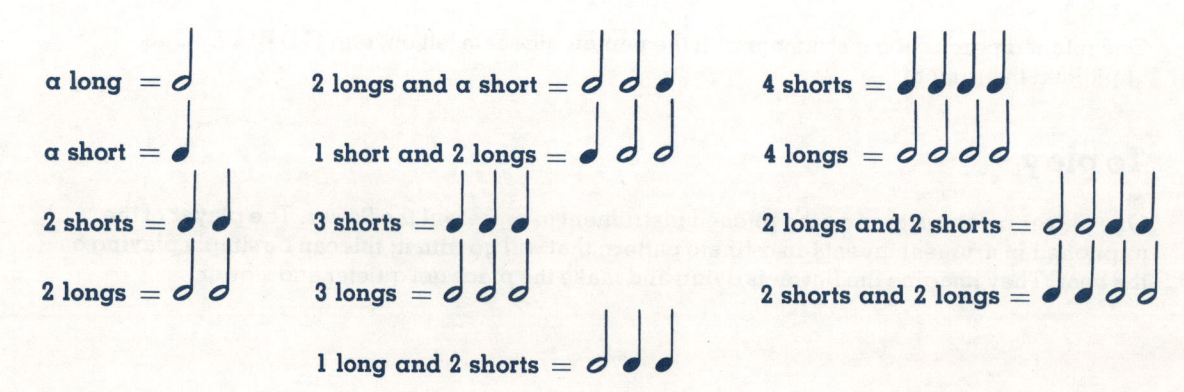

a long = 𝅗𝅥	2 longs and a short = 𝅗𝅥 𝅗𝅥 ♩	4 shorts = ♩♩♩♩
a short = ♩	1 short and 2 longs = ♩ 𝅗𝅥 𝅗𝅥	4 longs = 𝅗𝅥 𝅗𝅥 𝅗𝅥 𝅗𝅥
2 shorts = ♩♩	3 shorts = ♩♩♩	2 longs and 2 shorts = 𝅗𝅥 𝅗𝅥 ♩♩
2 longs = 𝅗𝅥 𝅗𝅥	3 longs = 𝅗𝅥 𝅗𝅥 𝅗𝅥	2 shorts and 2 longs = ♩♩ 𝅗𝅥 𝅗𝅥
	1 long and 2 shorts = 𝅗𝅥 ♩♩	

36 4 short and 2 long sounds	37 Sounds getting slower and louder	38 Sounds getting faster and louder	39 Sounds getting faster and softer	40 Sounds getting slower and softer
35 2 long and 2 short sounds	34 4 short and 4 long sounds	33 1 long and 2 short sounds	32 1 short and 2 long sounds	31 3 long sounds
26 Joined together sounds (legato)	27 A pattern with 2 beats in a bar	28 A pattern with 3 beats in a bar	29 A pattern with no beat	30 3 short sounds
25 Separated sounds (staccato)	24 2 long and 1 short sound	23 2 short and 1 long sound	22 2 long sounds	21 2 short sounds
16 Soft slow sounds	17 A short loud sound	18 A short soft sound	19 A long loud sound	20 A long soft sound
15 Soft fast sounds	14 Loud slow sounds	13 Loud fast sounds	12 Sounds getting gradually slower	11 Sounds getting gradually faster
6 A short sound	7 An interesting sound	8 A steady beat	9 Sounds getting louder	10 Sounds getting softer
5 A long sound	4 Slow sounds	3 Fast sounds	2 A loud sound	1 A soft sound

Opposites

These games explore various musical concepts.

Number of players

These games are all to be played in pairs.

Age 6—13

Fast and Slow

Objective

To understand fast and slow.

Materials

None

To play

Number the pair 1 and 2. Player 1 claps a rhythm fast. Player 2 claps it slowly. After several rounds change over.

Loud and Quiet

Objective

To understand loud and quiet.

Materials

A simple unpitched percussion instrument for each child.

To play

This game can be played without instruments by using a two-finger clap for quiet and a whole hand clap for loud.
Number the pair 1 and 2. Player 1 claps or plays a rhythm loudly and player 2 echoes it quietly. After several rounds change over.

Combination

Objective

To distinguish between loud and quiet and fast and slow.

Materials

A simple unpitched percussion instrument for each child.

To play

Number the pair 1 and 2. Player 1 plays or claps a rhythm loud and slow. Player 2 imitates it quiet and fast. Then player 1 plays quiet and fast and player 2 imitates the rhythm loud and slow. Repeat this for the other combination of sounds: loud and fast and quiet and slow.

High and Low

Objective

To distinguish between high and low.

Materials

An instrument capable of playing high and low, e.g. glockenspiel, xylophone.

To play

Number the pair 1 and 2. Player 1 plays a pattern high and player 2 plays it low. After several rounds change round.

High and Low (with movement)

Objective

To distinguish between high and low.

Materials

An instrument capable of playing high and low. A head scarf.

To play

Number the pair 1 and 2. Player 1 plays a pattern high while player 2 waves his scarf in time high above his head. Player 1 plays the pattern low while player 2 makes patterns with it on the floor. After several rounds change over.

Composition games

Conversations

Objective

To introduce the idea of responding musically to another person and being sensitive and aware of their musical expression (this links up later on to the idea of balancing phrases).

Number of players 4—30

Age 5—9

Materials

Two contrasting instruments, e.g. a drum and a wood block.

To play

The children sit in a circle. The two instruments are passed round in opposite directions while the class sings:

[Musical notation: Con-ver-sa-tions, con-ver-sa-tions, What shall we say to-day?]

The two children who have the instruments when the song finishes have a musical conversation on their instruments, one child playing first and then the other. The children will need guidance on how to answer one another; they should not just imitate the other one but listen carefully and make a musical response. It might help to talk about it initially — a calm statement can be followed by an angry one or by another calm one or a sad one and so on. Such discussion is unnecessary later when the children have the feel of 'talking' musically. Each child also needs to be aware of when the preceding one has finished, so that he does not 'butt in'.

Acky, Acky Alphabet

Objective

To explore unusual vocal sounds.

Number of players 4—30

Age 5—11

Materials

None.

To play

Each child takes a letter of the alphabet in turn and invents a sound for it. The first child invents a sound for 'A' and says, e.g. 'A is ACKY ACKY.' Then the first child says 'A is ACKY ACKY again followed by the second child who adds one for 'B', e.g. 'B is BLURP'. The first child says 'A is ACKY ACKY', the second 'B is BLURP' and the third child adds 'C is CRRRR.' The players progress through the alphabet in this way, each time repeating all the previous letters and sounds.

If the end of the alphabet is reached before all the players have been included, they can
a) start again with the new children inventing new sounds; or
b) use little 'a' etc when the pupil with the little 'a' does the same sound as the first (big) 'A', but softer, e.g. ACKY ACKY becomes acky acky; or
c) use double 'A', when the pupil with double 'A' does the single 'A' sound twice.

Variation

A simpler version is to use just pure sounds, e.g. A is a raspberry blown, B is a whistle, C is a hum, and so on.

Geographical Music

Objective

To make up pieces in small groups using rhythmic ostinati.

Number of players 8—32

Age 8—13

Materials

One instrument for each member of the class, although the game can be played with clapping only. A large room. A set of cards as shown opposite, with enough for one for each player. (The cards are in groups of four, but a fifth one has been provided in some sets to allow for situations in which the number playing is not divisible by four).

To play

Shuffle the cards and give them out, one to each player. The players arrange themselves (by asking each other) into their geographical groups.

The players in each group choose their instruments and are sent somewhere where they can make up their piece.

Each group decides how to construct its piece — whether everyone starts together or one after the other, whether each plays his own rhythm or whether all four (or five) rhythms are joined together to make one long rhythm (which can be played by each instrument in turn, or in canon, or all together), how to bring it to a close, and so on.

When the pieces are completed all are heard and commented on.

Variations

1 The class might discuss the characteristics of the music of the country involved and try to incorporate some of these characteristics into their piece, e.g. syncopation in the USA piece.
2 The principle of dividing into sets in this way may be used for any subject that the class happens to be studying.

St. Giles Cathedral			
Houses of Parliament			

Princes Street	Buckingham Palace	Pyramids	Bourbon Street	Lenin's Tomb	Lorelei	Gladesville Bridge	Taj Mahal

Edinburgh	London	Cairo	New Orleans	Moscow	St. Goar	Sydney	Agra

Forth	Thames	Nile	Mississippi	Volga	Rhine	Parramatta	Ganges

Scotland	England	Egypt	USA	USSR	Germany	Australia	India

Musical Telegrams

Objective

To make up a piece in small groups using a pentatonic scale.

Number of players 4—32

Age 8—13

Materials

One instrument for each member of the class. Each group must have one pitched instrument capable of playing the chosen pentatonic scale and one child capable of playing it. A pencil and paper for each group.

To play

The objective of this game is to compose a telegram of a given number of words which is sent to and played by the members of another group. The telegrams can consist of any number of words up to eight.

Divide the players into groups of two to four. Decide how many words the telegram is to have, e.g. four, and the scale to be used, e.g. CDEGA.

Each group composes a telegram of the given number of words, using words that begin with the notes of a pentatonic scale; CDEGA is a good one to use, and an example of a telegram using this scale would be 'Great Granny Dead Already'. The telegram is passed to the next group which takes the initial letters of the words as the basis of an ostinato for the pitched instrument, e.g. Great Granny Dead Already = GGDA. The players can choose the rhythm for it but they should keep it simple. One of the other instruments takes the rhythm of the pitched part, e.g.

Great granny dead already

♩ ♫ ♫ ♫

The other instruments are free to do as they think appropriate. They too can take the word rhythm, perhaps one after the other or in canon. The pitched part should underlie the whole piece but otherwise the group is free to make its own piece in its own way, deciding how to start and finish, etc.

When the pieces are completed all are heard and commented on.

Variation

This game can be used for any group of notes, the whole major scale, for example.

Sally Beetle

Objective

To create a piece inspired by geometric shapes and in so doing explore various musical concepts.

Number of players 6—30

Age 9—13

Materials

Enough instruments for each player to have one. Some in each group can clap and some have simple instruments like paper rustles and sandpaper sheets. Sally Beetles cut out of cardboard as shown (each in a different colour if possible). There should be one Sally Beetle for each group of players.
A dice.

To play

Each group aims to build up a Sally Beetle by throwing the dice and interpreting the appropriate shape in sound.

Divide the players into groups of six. Each member of the group will take on one part of Sally Beetle, i.e. one for the hat, one for the head, one for each arm, one for the body, one for a leg and one for a foot. Each group decides how to 'draw' each of the parts in sound. The first time it is probably a good idea to give the children ideas on how to do this; the following ideas are suggestions: the leg is a long rectangle so use long sounds for it; the arm is a short rectangle so use short sounds. As both these patterns have four sides the patterns could have four beats in a bar, e.g.

There are three triangles. These could be three patterns with three beats in a bar. The small feet triangles could be played softly, the middle-sized hat played moderately loud and the large body played loud, e.g.

Foot 3/4 (soft) ♩ ♩ ♩ | ♫ ♩ ♩ | ♩ ♩ ♩ | ♩. ‖ Hand drum

Hat 3/4 (moderately loud) ♩ ♩ ♩ | ♫ ♩ ♩ | ♩ ♩ ♩ | ♩. ‖ Claves

Body 3/4 (loud) ♩ ♩ ♩ | ♫ ♩ ♩ | ♩ ♩ ♩ | ♩. ‖ Big tambour

The round head as it has no sides could be a pattern without a steady beat, e.g.

Head 𝅗𝅥 − 𝄾 ♩ ♩ 𝄾 ♩ − 𝅗𝅥 ‖ Triangle

Each group in turn throws the dice. They collect the part of the Sally Beetle corresponding with the number of the dice. 1 = leg, 2 = foot, 3 = head, 4 = arm, 5 = hat, 6 = body. When they have collected the appropriate part they play their piece. As the parts are added the piece will get longer and the various patterns are added together; so that a group which has collected a head, a body, one leg and one foot might play: e.g.

Cymbal
Big tambour 3/4 ♩ ♩ ♩ (loud) | ♫ ♩ ♩ | ♩ ♩ ♩ | ♩. | | | | 4/4 𝅗𝅥 𝅗𝅥 | 𝅝 | 𝅗𝅥 𝅗𝅥 | 𝅝
Hand drum   ♩ ♩ ♩ | ♫ ♩ ♩ | ♩ ♩ ♩ | ♩. |
Triangle (soft)   𝅗𝅥 − 𝄾 ♩ ♩ 𝄾 − 𝅗𝅥 |

At the end each group should play a piece incorporating all the parts in any order they choose.

Variation

As the children get used to the game they will invent their own ways of interpreting the shapes in the sound. They will need to think about how to join the various patterns together satisfactorily. They may not want to have the patterns one after the other as suggested here, but have some of them simultaneously. This game can be a good exercise in creating a longer musical piece.

Chordal Adventure

Objective

To explore the three primary chords in the key of C.

Number of players 6—30

Age 9—13

Materials

Three boards as illustrated opposite. Sufficient pitched instruments for each child to be able to have a share on one (for example, there can be at least two and possibly three children on each pitched percussion instrument and more on the piano). A pointer (attached with Blu-tak) that will move round each board. One dice for each of the three groups.

To play

Divide the class into three groups. Seat the children so that each member of the group can see his own group's board clearly. Appoint one member of each group to be in charge of the dice and the pointer.

Make sure that each member of each group can find on his instrument all the notes on his particular board. If children are sharing a pitched percussion instrument give each player one note only in each chord.

All groups start together. The thrower in each group throws the dice and moves the pointer through the appropriate number of squares. The members of the group play the note indicated on that square. The thrower then throws again, and so on. The boards are designed so that the chord will gradually change from C E G to F A C to G B D to C E G.

It may be helpful for the teacher to keep a steady beat going on a drum. At first children can be told to play in time with this. When they are used to the game you might leave them free to make up whatever pattern they like on the notes (see Variation below). It is very important that the whole piece progresses without talking.

Variation

You can make a more complex version of the board in which there is a note value on each square and the players are not only required to play the correct notes but to repeat them in the note value given on the square. In this case it will be very important that the teacher maintains a steady beat on a drum to which they can all relate.

Group 1

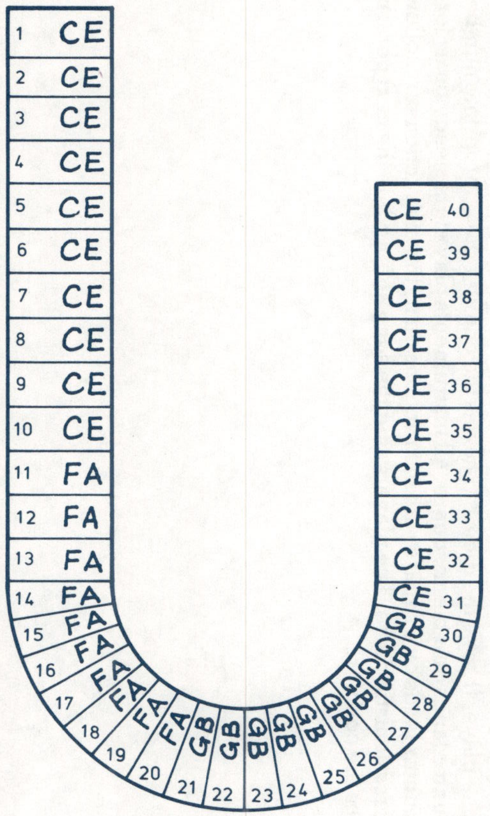

1	2	3	4	5	6	7	8	9	10	11	12	13	14	15	16	17	18	19	20	21	22	23	24	25	26	27	28	29	30	31	32	33	34	35	36	37	38	39	40
CE	CE	CE	CE	CE	CE	CE	CE	CE	CE	FA	FA	FA	FA	FA	FA	FA	FA	FA	GB	GB	GB	GB	GB	GB	GB	GB	GB	GB	GB	CE	CE	CE	CE	CE	CE	CE	CE	CE	CE

Group 2

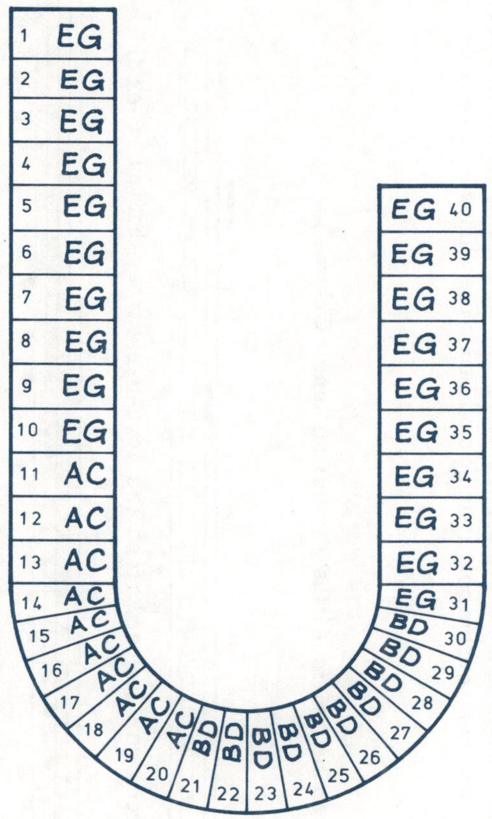

1	2	3	4	5	6	7	8	9	10	11	12	13	14	15	16	17	18	19	20	21	22	23	24	25	26	27	28	29	30	31	32	33	34	35	36	37	38	39	40
EG	EG	EG	EG	EG	EG	EG	EG	EG	EG	AC	AC	AC	AC	AC	AC	AC	AC	AC	AC	BD	BD	BD	BD	BD	BD	BD	BD	BD	BD	EG	EG	EG	EG	EG	EG	EG	EG	EG	EG

Group 3

1	2	3	4	5	6	7	8	9	10	11	12	13	14	15	16	17	18	19	20	21	22	23	24	25	26	27	28	29	30	31	32	33	34	35	36	37	38	39	40
CG	CG	CG	CG	CG	CG	CG	CG	CG	CG	FC	FC	FC	FC	FC	FC	FC	FC	FC	FC	GD	GD	GD	GD	GD	GD	GD	GD	GD	GD	CG	CG	CG	CG	CG	CG	CG	CG	CG	CG

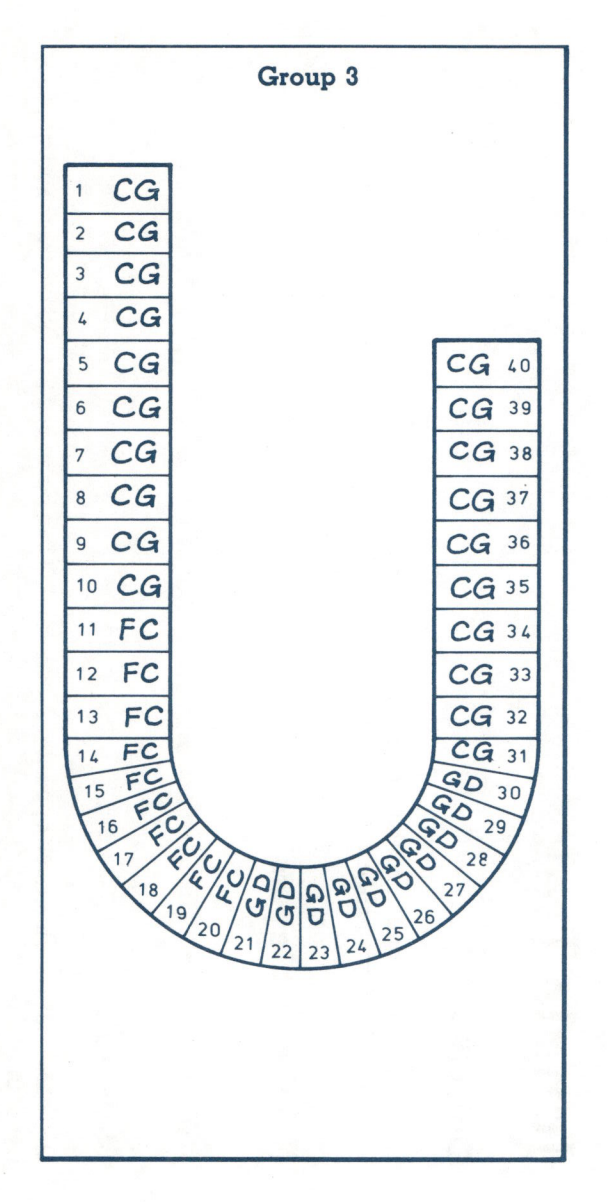

Jungle Trek

Objective

To create impressionistic sound pictures using rhythms.
To create a large piece like a rondo in structure.

Number of players 2—30

Age 6—13

Materials

One base board as illustrated opposite. A counter that can be moved around the track and stuck to it with Blu-tak.
A dice and shaker. A wide variety of percussion instruments: Indian cymbals, triangles, drums of various sizes, paper rustles, shakers, cymbal with beater and wire brush, claves, wood block, whistles, reso-reso scraper. (But the board can be modified to use whatever is available.)

To play

Give each player an instrument. All the players sing 'Jungle Calypso':

Cynthia Raza

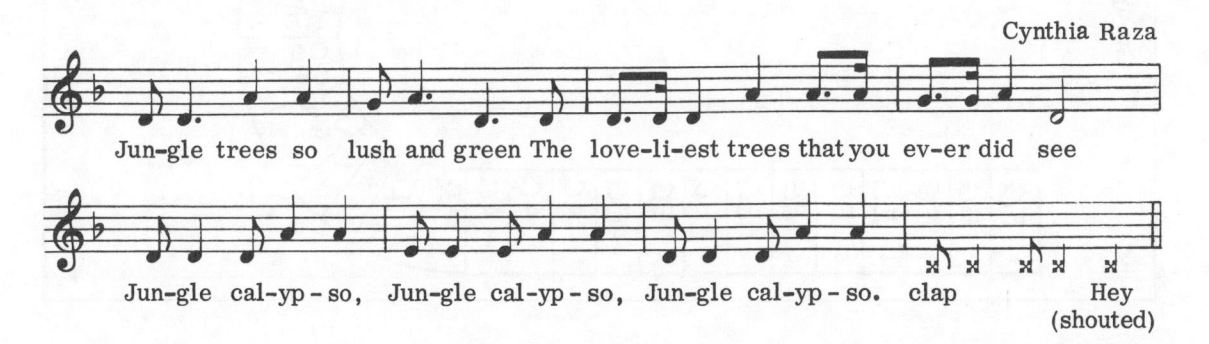

Jun-gle trees so lush and green The love-li-est trees that you ev-er did see

Jun-gle cal-yp-so, Jun-gle cal-yp-so, Jun-gle cal-yp-so. clap Hey (shouted)

During the song one player throws the dice and moves the counter the appropriate number of squares. If the counter lands on a blank square, all instruments play eight steady beats for safe trekking. If the counter lands on a square with instructions on it, the instructions are followed to create a short impressionistic piece. The players sing the song again while the next person throws the dice and moves the counter.

1	2 The jungle is very still. Make a pattern using paper rustles and shakers.	3	4 Creeper winds round trees. Make a winding pattern on scrapers and shakers.
8	7 Thick undergrowth. Use low instruments with lots of different rhythms at once.	6	5
9 Tall trees. Make a pattern consisting of scrapes on scraper or shakes on shaker or tambourine followed by a cymbal clash.	10 Rain falls. Make short sounds on metal and wooden instruments.	11	12 Monkeys swing from tree to tree. Make up a piece using a swinging rhythm ♩♪♪ on tambourines and claves.
16	15	14 Lions are heard. Make a pattern on drums of various kinds.	13
17 A mist descends. Make a piece using bells, Indian cymbals and humming long notes.	18 Leaves rustle overhead. Make up a piece using shakers, scrapers and paper rustles.	19 Multi-coloured birds perch in the trees. Make up a piece using whistles, triangles, wood blocks and claves.	20 A stream ripples by. Make a piece using bells, triangles and tambourines.
24	23 Swamp. Use deep drum and scraper.	22 Brightly coloured flowers. Make up a piece using Indian cymbals, cymbal with wire brushes and tambourines with flashes of colour.	21
25 Snakes glide past. Make up scraper patterns with a cymbal with wire brush and sss-sound.	26	27 Elephants stampede. Drum patterns getting gradually louder and faster and then slower and softer.	28 Herd of giraffes. Use scrapes on scraper and shakes on tambourine followed by a cymbal clash and drum beat.
32 A herd of deer rush past. Use running patterns on wooden instruments.	31	30 Wind rustles the trees. Use shakers and paper rustles.	29

The River

Objectives

To create small impressionistic sound pictures.
To create an overall piece of rondo structure.

Number of players 4—30

Age 6—13

Materials

One base board as illustrated opposite. A counter that can be moved round the track and stuck to it with Blu-tak. A dice and a shaker. Pitched instruments: chime bars, xylophones, glockenspiels, metallophone, recorders. Percussion instruments: Indian cymbals, triangle, drums of various sizes, tambour, paper rustles, shakers, cymbal with beater and wire brush, tambourines, claves, wood block, whistles, reso-reso scraper.
(The board can be modified to use whatever instruments are available.)

To play

Give each player an instrument. All the players sing this song:

Smetana adapted June Tillman

Chorus: The riv-er goes me-an-der-ing to and fro___ Past vil-lag-es and cot-tag-es See how it flows.

During the singing one player throws the dice and moves the counter the appropriate number of squares. If the counter lands on a blank square all instruments play the following to represent the swirling river:

If the counter lands on a square with instructions on it, the instructions are followed to create a short impressionistic piece.

The players sing the song again while the next person throws the dice and moves the counter.

Extension

You could follow this game by listening to Smetana's 'Vltava' on which the game is based. You could add a movement sequence to it.

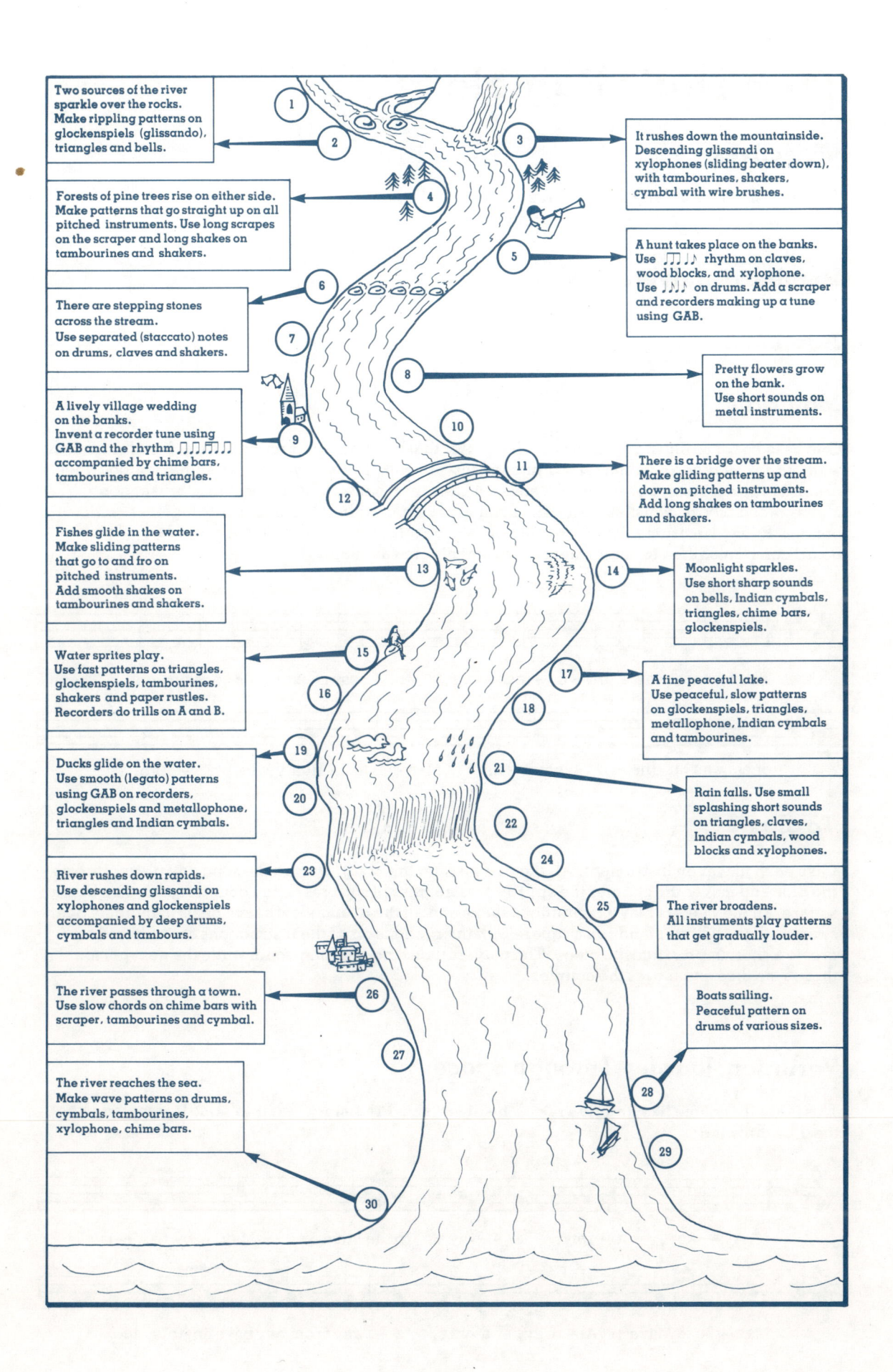

1, 2. **Two sources of the river sparkle over the rocks.** Make rippling patterns on glockenspiels (glissando), triangles and bells.

3. **It rushes down the mountainside.** Descending glissandi on xylophones (sliding beater down), with tambourines, shakers, cymbal with wire brushes.

4. **Forests of pine trees rise on either side.** Make patterns that go straight up on all pitched instruments. Use long scrapes on the scraper and long shakes on tambourines and shakers.

5. **A hunt takes place on the banks.** Use ♫♪ rhythm on claves, wood blocks, and xylophone. Use ♪♪♪ on drums. Add a scraper and recorders making up a tune using GAB.

6, 7. **There are stepping stones across the stream.** Use separated (staccato) notes on drums, claves and shakers.

8. **Pretty flowers grow on the bank.** Use short sounds on metal instruments.

9. **A lively village wedding on the banks.** Invent a recorder tune using GAB and the rhythm ♫♫♫ accompanied by chime bars, tambourines and triangles.

10, 11, 12. **There is a bridge over the stream.** Make gliding patterns up and down on pitched instruments. Add long shakes on tambourines and shakers.

13. **Fishes glide in the water.** Make sliding patterns that go to and fro on pitched instruments. Add smooth shakes on tambourines and shakers.

14. **Moonlight sparkles.** Use short sharp sounds on bells, Indian cymbals, triangles, chime bars, glockenspiels.

15, 16. **Water sprites play.** Use fast patterns on triangles, glockenspiels, tambourines, shakers and paper rustles. Recorders do trills on A and B.

17, 18. **A fine peaceful lake.** Use peaceful, slow patterns on glockenspiels, triangles, metallophone, Indian cymbals and tambourines.

19, 20. **Ducks glide on the water.** Use smooth (legato) patterns using GAB on recorders, glockenspiels and metallophone, triangles and Indian cymbals.

21, 22. **Rain falls.** Use small splashing short sounds on triangles, claves, Indian cymbals, wood blocks and xylophones.

23, 24. **River rushes down rapids.** Use descending glissandi on xylophones and glockenspiels accompanied by deep drums, cymbals and tambours.

25. **The river broadens.** All instruments play patterns that get gradually louder.

26, 27. **The river passes through a town.** Use slow chords on chime bars with scraper, tambourines and cymbal.

28, 29. **Boats sailing.** Peaceful pattern on drums of various sizes.

30. **The river reaches the sea.** Make wave patterns on drums, cymbals, tambourines, xylophone, chime bars.

Prehistoric Ramble

Objectives

To create small impressionistic sound pictures.
To create an overall piece of rondo structure.

Number of players 4—30

Age 6—13

Materials

One base board as illustrated opposite. A counter that can be moved round the track and stuck to it with Blu-tak. A dice and a shaker. Unpitched instruments: Indian cymbals, triangle, tambourines, drums of various sizes, bells, paper rustles, shakers, cymbal with beater and wire brush, gong, claves, wood blocks, whistles, reso-reso scraper, sandpaper block, stones stuck together, whip, bongos. Pitched instruments: piano, melodica, glockenspiel, metallophone, recorders. (The board can be modified to use whatever instruments area available.)

There once was a din-o-saur-us, -o-saur-us, -o-saur-us. There once was a din-o-saur-us Man-y mil-lion years a-go.

To play

Give each player an instrument. All the players sing this song. During the song one player throws the dice and moves the counter the appropriate number of squares. If the counter lands on a blank square, all the shakers play a continuous shake and all the drums slow heavy beats to indicate deep swamps. If the counter lands on a square with instructions on it, the instructions are followed to create a short impressionistic piece. The players then sing the song again while the next person throws the dice and moves the counter.

Variation: Journey Through Space

This is another game like 'Jungle Trek', 'The River' and 'Prehistoric Ramble'. Use this song during the dice throwing:

A-way, a-way, a-way to the stars, May-be to Ve-nus, May-be to Mars A-way, a-way, a-way from our base in-to space.

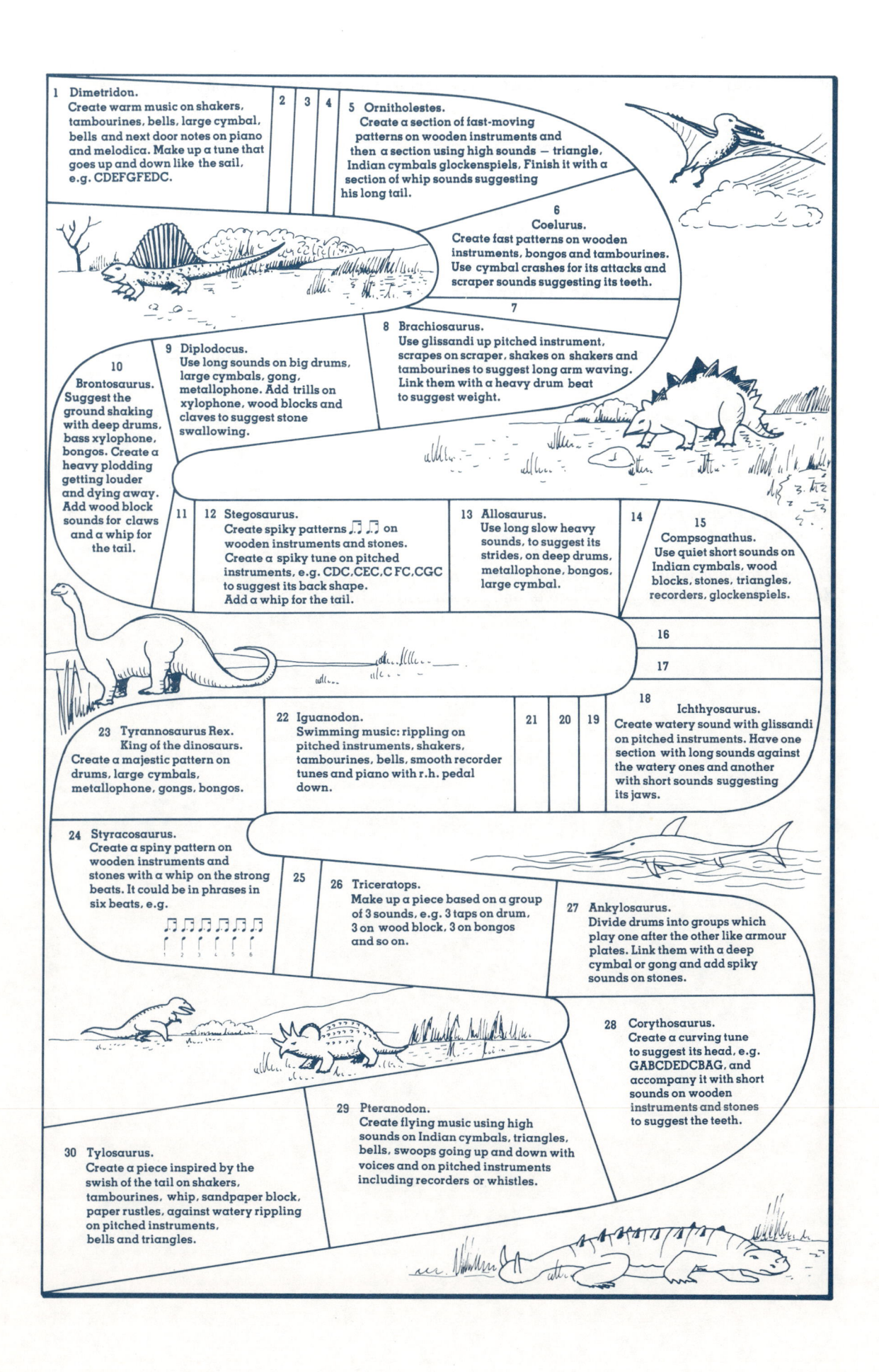

1 **Dimetridon.**
Create warm music on shakers, tambourines, bells, large cymbal, bells and next door notes on piano and melodica. Make up a tune that goes up and down like the sail, e.g. CDEFGFEDC.

2 3 4

5 **Ornitholestes.**
Create a section of fast-moving patterns on wooden instruments and then a section using high sounds — triangle, Indian cymbals glockenspiels, Finish it with a section of whip sounds suggesting his long tail.

6 **Coelurus.**
Create fast patterns on wooden instruments, bongos and tambourines. Use cymbal crashes for its attacks and scraper sounds suggesting its teeth.

7

8 **Brachiosaurus.**
Use glissandi up pitched instrument, scrapes on scraper, shakes on shakers and tambourines to suggest long arm waving. Link them with a heavy drum beat to suggest weight.

9 **Diplodocus.**
Use long sounds on big drums, large cymbals, gong, metallophone. Add trills on xylophone, wood blocks and claves to suggest stone swallowing.

10 **Brontosaurus.**
Suggest the ground shaking with deep drums, bass xylophone, bongos. Create a heavy plodding getting louder and dying away. Add wood block sounds for claws and a whip for the tail.

11

12 **Stegosaurus.**
Create spiky patterns ♫ ♫ on wooden instruments and stones. Create a spiky tune on pitched instruments, e.g. CDC,CEC,C FC,CGC to suggest its back shape. Add a whip for the tail.

13 **Allosaurus.**
Use long slow heavy sounds, to suggest its strides, on deep drums, metallophone, bongos, large cymbal.

14

15 **Compsognathus.**
Use quiet short sounds on Indian cymbals, wood blocks, stones, triangles, recorders, glockenspiels.

16

17

18 **Ichthyosaurus.**
Create watery sound with glissandi on pitched instruments. Have one section with long sounds against the watery ones and another with short sounds suggesting its jaws.

19 20 21

22 **Iguanodon.**
Swimming music: rippling on pitched instruments, shakers, tambourines, bells, smooth recorder tunes and piano with r.h. pedal down.

23 **Tyrannosaurus Rex.**
King of the dinosaurs. Create a majestic pattern on drums, large cymbals, metallophone, gongs, bongos.

24 **Styracosaurus.**
Create a spiny pattern on wooden instruments and stones with a whip on the strong beats. It could be in phrases in six beats, e.g.
♫♫♫♫♫♫
1 2 3 4 5 6

25

26 **Triceratops.**
Make up a piece based on a group of 3 sounds, e.g. 3 taps on drum, 3 on wood block, 3 on bongos and so on.

27 **Ankylosaurus.**
Divide drums into groups which play one after the other like armour plates. Link them with a deep cymbal or gong and add spiky sounds on stones.

28 **Corythosaurus.**
Create a curving tune to suggest its head, e.g. GABCDEDCBAG, and accompany it with short sounds on wooden instruments and stones to suggest the teeth.

29 **Pteranodon.**
Create flying music using high sounds on Indian cymbals, triangles, bells, swoops going up and down with voices and on pitched instruments including recorders or whistles.

30 **Tylosaurus.**
Create a piece inspired by the swish of the tail on shakers, tambourines, whip, sandpaper block, paper rustles, against watery rippling on pitched instruments, bells and triangles.

83

Make up your own board and instructions for the pieces of music. Here are some suggestions:

Rocket taking off
Rising glissandi on pitched instruments.

Sense of weightlessness
A piece with no beat using isolated notes on softer instruments — shakers, triangles, Indian cymbals, fingers scratching on drum surfaces, cymbal with wire brushes.

A new sun appears
Sudden flashes on cymbal, shaker, tambourines, claves, wood blocks and next door notes on a melodica.
Bleeps from computer control
Make up a piece using vocal sounds like blip, bleep in various rhythms. Create a pattern, e.g.

♩ | ♪ ♪ ♪ | ♩ ♩ | ♩ ||

and say it in canon.
Robot music
A city on a strange planet
A radiation belt
Solar energy
The heat through which a space ship passes on re-entering the Earth's atmosphere.
You could listen to Holst's 'The Planets' and use some ideas from it.

Glossary

Antiphonal The contrast between two different sound groups. In the game 'Somebody's knocking at your door' antiphonal means the contrast between a solo voice and a group of voices.

Bar A group of beats with an accent on the first. Bars are divided from each other by bar lines which cause a regular accent, .
e.g. ♩♩♩♩ is the same as ♩♩|♩♩

In this book most bars contain either two beats, three beats or four beats.

Beat The underlying pulse of the music.

Binary A two-part form in which the second section is different from the first and is often described as AB (A being the first section and B the second).

Body rhythm Rhythms made by parts of the body, e.g. knee slap, finger click, tapping head, clapping, stamping.

Canon A piece in which one person has a tune which is then sung or played by another person before the first person has finished. Rhythms can also be performed in canon, e.g.

A canon is like a round.

Chord A group of notes sounding together (see primary chords).

Clef A sign giving the five lines on which music is normally written (the stave) their meaning. The two in common use are treble 𝄞 and bass 𝄢:

The treble clef makes the notes on the stave thus:

C D E F G A B C D E F G A

The bass clef make the notes on the stave thus:

E F G A B C D E F G A B C

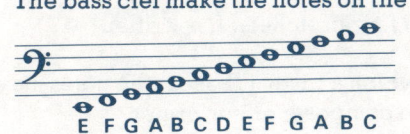

Crotchets A rhythmic unit, written ♩♩ ; crotchets are sometimes described at elementary level as 'walking notes'.

Glissando The sound produced by sliding the beater along a pitched instrument or a finger along the piano keyboard. A glissando can go up (╱) or down (╲) or up and down (⌢).

Key The scale which a piece of music uses.

Legato Notes performed in a smooth style without a break.

Minim A rhythmic unit equalling two crotchets. Sometimes called 'jumping notes' at elementary level. It is written ♩

Notation Any method of writing music down. The most common uses the stave of five lines (see staff notation), but it is possible to draw sounds in a graphic notation, e.g. ∿ for shake, ╱ for a glissando up.

Ostinato A repeated pattern, which can be pitched or purely rhythmic.

Pentatonic scale A major scale with the 4th and 7th notes removed; the pentatonic scale starting on the note C is CDEGA.

Phrase A group of bars. A phrase can consist of any number of bars but often consists of two, four or eight bars grouped together e.g. ♩♩│♫♩│♫♫│♩

Pitched instrument An instrument capable of producing sounds of a definite pitch, e.g. CDEFGABC, and on which a tune can be played.

Primary chords The three-note chords based on the first, fourth and fifth notes of the major scale. In the scale of C major they are CEG, FAC and GBD.

Quavers A rhythmic unit that is half a crotchet. Sometimes called 'running notes' at elementary level. They are written ♪♪ and ♫

Rests Periods of silence within a piece of music. They are written thus:

semibreve rest   minim rest   crotchet rest   quaver rest

Rhythm The rhythmic pattern of a piece of music.

Rondo A musical form in which one section recurs, so that it is sometimes written as ABACADA etc., in which A is the first section, B the second section, A returns, followed by a new section C and so on.

Scale A pattern of notes, e.g. the major scale of C is CDEFGABC with a gap of a semitone between E and F and B and C.

Score All the parts that sound together written one under the other.

Semibreve A rhythmic unit equalling four crotchets. It is written 𝅝

Series A set of pitched notes on which a piece is based; the notes may be played in any rhythm at the choice of the composer or performer.

Staff notation A method of writing music down on five lines, using signs for the various note values and rests, e.g.

Staccato Perform music with the notes detached.

Time signature   The two figures at the beginning of a piece of music to the right of the clef that denote the number of beats in a bar and the kind of note that is the beat. The ones used in this book are

$\frac{2}{4}$ 2 crotchets in a bar

$\frac{3}{4}$ 3 crotchets in a bar

$\frac{4}{4}$ 4 crotchets in a bar, sometimes written as C — common time.

List of instruments

Beaters
Many kinds are available and it is good to have as great a variety as possible. Some examples are:
Padded felt These can be made by covering cotton headed washing up mops with a piece of material. There are many types on the market of varying degrees of softness.

Rubber Sold originally to go with chime bars, they can be used on other instruments as well.
Wooden There are two types. One is round headed for use with glockenspiels and wood blocks, and can be bought with a rubber head on one end and a wooden on the other. The other type is straight:

for use with drums and you can use dowelling for these.
Metal These are supplied with triangles but also make interesting effects on xylophones and glockenspiels, teacups or glasses.
Hands These can be used flat or can scratch the surface of a drum. Fingers used separately can produce rhythms.

Bell
There is a wide variety on the market, including those used as ornaments, small bells which have a tongue, big bells like fire bells and school bells which can be played rhythmically by holding the tongue and striking them with a triangle beater. There are also clusters of *sleighbells,* which can be played rhythmically by holding them in one hand and tapping one handle with the other.

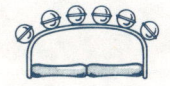

Cowbells can be struck (see also Indian cymbals).

A set of small *tubular bells* makes a beautiful sound.

Bongos
These are pairs of small drums of different sizes and therefore of different pitches; it is better to buy tunable ones as their heads can be replaced. They are played with the hands or fingers and can perform complicated rhythms.

Castanets
The easiest to operate have two wooden flaps joined with a piece of elastic (which acts as a spring).

Others have one (better) or more flaps mounted on a wooden handle.

The Spanish finger kind are very difficult to operate.

Chime bars
These consist of metal strips (there are some wooden ones available too) mounted on wooden resonators. They are sold in pitched sets.

They make a bell-like sound when struck with the rubber beater supplied with them but other effects are obtainable with different beaters. They are useful in that they can be split up and divided among the class in chordal groups.

Claves
Two hardwood sticks which are struck together

There are also rhythm sticks which are cheap imitations and can be made from dowelling.

Cymbals
It is worth buying a good cymbal made of spun steel (the rings from the machine turning can be seen). Cheaper ones are very tinny and two saucepan lids will do as well. You can use a variety of beaters on them and hit them at various points (middle, edge, etc.) to produce a variety of sounds. Pairs can be clashed together or a single cymbal can be mounted on a stand. An unusual effect can be obtained by rubbing a violin or cello bow across the edge of the cymbal:

There are small *finger cymbals* that give a higher pitched sound.

Drums
There are many different kinds available. Most useful are the *tambours* that are like tambourines without the jingles. Try to get these with tuning pegs and in a variety of sizes which will produce different notes, and to have one really large one (50cm) that will give a deep note, or invest in a *bass drum*. *Side drums* or *snare drums* are double sided and have wires stretched across one of the skins to give a distinctive sharp quality. You can produce a similar sound by stretching strips of shells, beans or beads over a drum skin lashed to a wooden bowl or box. Home-made drums can be made by stretching vellum or rubber inner tube across a tin and lashing it with cord round the side of the tin, the bigger the tin the thicker the skin required. Two heads can be lashed together. A variety of sounds can be produced on drums by using different beaters or scratching fingers or sandpaper over the surface (see wire brushes).

Glockenspiel
A pitched instrument on which the bars are made of thin steel. Good ones produce a clear ringing sound but cheap ones can be very tinny. (See also pitched instruments)

Indian cymbals or Indian bells
These consists of a pair of heavy brass cymbals of small diameter which produce a high ringing bell-like sound when struck together.

Maracas
These are made out of gourds or hollowed out wood filled with seeds or other small objects. They are played in pairs. They are easily cracked and then their sound is poor (see also shakers).

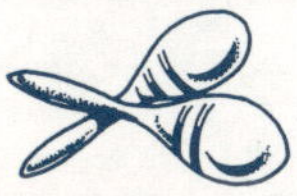

Melodica
A relation of the accordion with reeds and a piano keyboard, it comes in various sizes, can play melodies and simple chords and has a very strident tone. It can be played like a piano flat on a surface with a tube leading from the mouthpiece to the player's mouth.

Metallophone
This is a pitched instrument (see pitched instruments) with a resonating box like a xylophone but with large, thick steel keys. It has a gentle bell-like sound and is a great favourite. The glissando is especially beautiful.

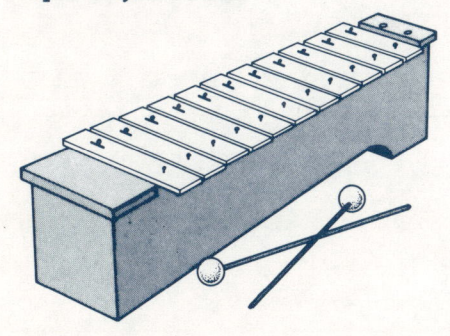

Paper rustles
Various types of paper will produce different rustling sounds — tissue, polythene, cellophane, greaseproof and so on. Dry leaves can also be used and milk bottle tops on the end of pieces of string attached to a pole can be shaken.

Piano
This can produce a wide variety of effects. If you expose the strings you can run fingers over them like a harp. Next door notes held down by a flat hand or forearm with the right hand pedal down ('note clusters') are useful. As it is often the only instrument in the school capable of producing a low sound it can be used for ostinato patterns low down. Several players can use it at once.

Pitched instruments
This term includes all instruments capable of producing notes of a definite pitch, so it includes glockenspiels, metallophones, xylophones, recorders, pianos, melodica, guitars and so on. Some of these instrument come in different sizes (glockenspiels, metallophones, xylophones, recorders, melodicas) the pitch varying with the size. The *glockenspiels, metallophones* and *xylophones* have removable bars or keys so you can leave on only a few notes if you want the children's choice to be limited (e.g. when using the pentatonic scale). These instruments also come in diatonic and chromatic versions. The diatonic (adequate for most school work) has one row of notes (the white notes of the piano) and is usually supplied with a F♯ bar and a B♭ bar that you can put on in place of F or B to play in G or F. The chromatic version has two rows of notes (both the black and white notes on the piano). On all these barred instruments you can run a beater along the bars to give a glissando effect that children love.

Recorder
It is good to have a variety of sizes: soprano, descant, treble, tenor, bass. Apart from being very useful for playing melodies (even with a very limited number of notes), recorders can also produce a variety of whistle effects from the mouthpiece alone, trills (alternating two next door notes) and tremolos (alternating two notes further apart).

Reso-reso scraper or guivo
This is a wide-diameter gourd or piece of bamboo with notches cut in the side. A bone or wooden stick is scraped along these notches to give a special sound quite unlike any other instrument. The tone varies with the speed of the scrape. You can make the bamboo version.

Sandpaper sheets
These can be rubbed together but last longer and can be played more rhythmically if mounted on blocks of wood.

Scraper
See Reso-reso Scraper.

Shakers
These come in a variety of shapes, sizes and with a variety of fillings — sand, seeds, lead shot, rice, stones. They are easily home-made from containers in a variety of material, such as wood (bamboo), plastic, cardboard, metal, and a variety of fillings, such as gravel, sugar, beans, pins, ball-bearings.

Stringed instruments
Use whatever you have available — violins, cellos, guitars, harp, auto harp.

Stones
Stones and shells can be hit together rhythmically. Different sizes will produce different pitches.

Tambourines
If the vellum head breaks the remaining ring of jingles can be struck rhythmically against the hand. Avoid the tinny sounding toy tambourines.

Triangle
Different sizes give different tone colours. Rapid rhythms are difficult to play but are easier in the angles.

Whip
The orchestral whip is two pieces of wood joined by a hinge and brought together smartly to give a whip-lash sound. Two strips of lino will suffice in class.

Whistles
There is a wide variety of these from *referee's whistle* to *tin whistle* or *flageolet* that resemble recorders in having holes than can be covered to make different notes.

A *Swanee Whistle* has a sliding stopper in its tube which can be gradually pushed in or drawn out causing a gradual slide up or down in pitch. (The headjoint of the recorder is a whistle, see recorders.)

Wire brushes
These can be used on drums and cymbals to give interesting effects. You can make a similar effect by tying together a bunch of twigs.

Wood block
This takes two forms. One is a wooden box with a slit cut in the side and struck with a wooden stick; sometimes there are two slits, one each side, each side producing a differently pitched note. The other form is cylindrical and is sometimes held on a handle.

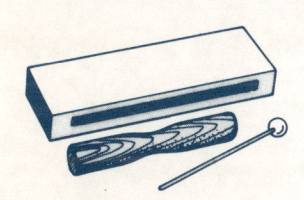

Xylophone
This consists of wooden keys mounted on a resonator box. A bass one is very useful. (See pitched instruments.)

Bibliography

Books of games or containing several games:

Addison, R. 1979 *Rhythm and Tune: Eighteen Classroom Games and Creative Projects for Young Children* (Chappell)

Dobbs, J. et al, 1980 *Ears and Eyes* Teacher's Book Two (Oxford University Press) Some games for upper juniors.

Gilbert, G. 1979 *Music is for Everyone: Games Book* (Mel Bay Publications, 4 Industrial Drive, Industrial Park, Pacific, Missouri 63069, USA) Games for young pianists

Gilbert, J. 1980 *Topic Anthologies for Young Children* (Oxford University Press) Some games for infants

Kurtag, G. *Jatekok Games for Piano* Vols 1-4 (Boosey & Hawkes/Editio Musica Budapest) Games using contemporary techniques.

Lee, J. *Group Piano Lessons — a practical guide* (Forsyth Brothers) Games for young pianists

Taylor, D. *A Directory of Musical Games* (Institute of Education, London University)

Taylor, D. 1976 *Dancing Rhymes, Singing Rhymes* and *Skipping Rhymes* from Learning with Traditional Rhymes series (Ladybird Books)

Tillman, J. *Kokoleoko* (Macmillan Education) Suggestions for the extension of composition activities with songs

Tillman, J. *Exploring Sound* (Stainer & Bell) Suggestions for extension of the composition activities

Tillman, J. and Braley, B. *New Horizons* (Stainer & Bell) Suggestions for extensions of the composition activities with songs

Winter, G. 1967 *Musical Instruments in the Classroom* (Longman) Some games for 10—14 year olds

Wiseman, H. and Northcote, S. *The Clarendon Book of Singing Games* Books 1 and 2 (Oxford University Press)

Wishart, T. 1975 *Sounds Fun* Books 1 and 2 (Schools Council Music in the Secondary School Project, University of York)

Published Games

Clap a Rhythm — a bingo type game and *Treble Clef Game* — note learning game.
Available from Barton-Griswold Publishing, PO Box 50607, Palo Alto, California 94303, USA.

Con Moto (Lawrence Glover) — a note and symbol learning game.
Available from Bayley & Ferguson Ltd, Sovereign House, 65 Berkely Street, Glasgow.

Several games by Sue Johnson for teaching note reading and learning musical symbols. Available from Alexander Brode Inc, 225 West 57th Street, New York, NY 10019, USA.

Play the Composers (Carolyn Maines) — a card game about musical appreciation and history.
Available from Dabco, PO Box 1772, Lynnwood, WA 98036, USA.

Allegro (Barbara Bonner-Morgan) — a board game to teach note value and composers and their works. Distributed in the UK by Boosey & Hawkes, 295 Regent Street, London W1.

Music Box — four music reading games.
Available from Wendy Max, 6 Wildwood Road, London NW11 6TB.

Music Dominoes and Music Playing Cards — two games for teaching notation.
Available from G Center, 79 Berkely Street, Glasgow.

Pick-a-Rhythm (Patricia and Michael Nyman) — large cards for teaching rhythm.
Available from Pamino Publications, Redan House, Redan Place, London W2.

A large number of games for teaching notation, musical symbols and facts about music. Available from Rhythm Bank Inc, PO Box 126, Fort Worth, Texas 76101, USA.